A Generous Impulse

A Generous Impulse

THE STORY OF GEORGE SWEETING

JERRY B. JENKINS

Library of Congress Cataloging-in-Publication Data

Jenkins, Jerry B.
    A generous impulse / by Jerry Jenkins.
        p. cm.
    Rev. ed., originally published in 1987.
    ISBN 0-8024-4024-X
    1. Sweeting, George, 1924- 2. Clergy–United States–Biography. 3. Evangelists–United States–Biography. 4. Moody Bible Institute– Presidents–Biography. I. Title

BR1725.S89 J46 2001
269'.2'092–dc21
[B]
                                                        2001044431

1 3 5 7 9 10 8 6 4 2
Printed in the United States of America

To Hilda and the boys:
George, Jim, Don, and Bob

Contents

"Seldom repress a generous impulse."

GEORGE SWEETING

*"When we come to the end of life, the test will be,
How much have we given? Not, How much have we gotten?"*

GEORGE SWEETING

sweeting *noun* 1: a variety of sweet apple 2: archaic variation of sweetheart

Acknowledgments

$\mathcal{T}$ he Rev. Doctor Donald William Sweeting, George Sweeting's son, played a vital role in the preparation of this work. With a lifelong interest in his family history, Don—who pastors the Cherry Creek Presbyterian Church in Englewood, Colorado—interviewed several relatives of both parents, including some who have since died.

In 1978 Don wrote a college term paper entitled "The Germanic-Scot Connection/The American Experiences of Two Early Twentieth Century Immigrant Families." As late as last year, he interviewed more family members and childhood acquaintances of his parents in New Jersey and Pennsylvania.

I am indebted to Don for his cooperation and for the material gleaned from his work. Thanks also to Sherry Fischer for tape transcriptions and to Charlotte Arman for help on the manuscript preparation process.

1

Full Circle: Roots and Routes

During his sixteen years as president and twelve years as chancellor of the Moody Bible Institute of Chicago, George Sweeting looked like someone the board of trustees put together from a kit.

He was tall and trim with clear blue eyes, and his wavy hair matured from gold to brown to gray and, finally, to white. The second son and third child of six born to immigrant Scots, he embarked on a course of leadership from his youth. To the world he appeared a consummate commander and trailblazer.

He sang, he painted and drew, he preached, he wrote, he traveled the world as a soul-winning evangelist, he pastored, and he became the sixth president—and eventually chancellor—of the Moody Bible Institute. He married his childhood sweetheart and raised four handsome sons.

It may seem to outsiders that everything he touches turns to gold, but George Sweeting is also a man accustomed to struggle and hardship. In fact, for every outward appearance that makes him seem saintly, there is a corresponding private trait that proves his humanness.

For instance, his public, platform dignity is offset by a sense of humor that is boyish.

Balancing his highly visible role as a pastor, evangelist, college president, and conference speaker is his intense, private nature.

His personal spirituality is consistent and deep both in public and in private, but it is not sissified and does not detract from his being a man's man.

He is known to be humble, yet confident.

Friends and relatives know him to hate controversy and confrontation; coworkers and subordinates see him as superb in the face of both.

As a father he is both affectionate and distant, doting although still frequently addressing his grown boys as "Son."

Despite his public warmth and ease in formal situations, even his closest friends and confidants get only so near. Except for certain lifetime friends, even apparently intimate friends call him Doc.

Thoroughly competitive, George is a good loser, a brother says, but he can also be a gloating winner.

He sees himself to be not as patient as his wife, quicker to get to the bottom line, less of a listener. She balances him by reflecting those opposite qualities.

His preaching is simple, yet his message and its effect are profound.

Robust and healthy in his seventies, he has had two brushes with cancer and has privately struggled with stress-induced chest pains and other tension-related maladies.

George Sweeting is unabashedly image conscious, yet even his detractors don't attack his character.

Love has been a theme of his ministry since the beginning, and if there is one trait most frequently recognized by associates, family, and friends, it is his generosity. He admits that he can be openhanded to a fault. Even those with whom he has had grave differences are not able to find fault with him later.

If it is true that the child is father to the man, then to understand what made George Sweeting the complex man that he is requires a study of both his roots and his routes. Those who believe the story behind a silver-tongued, white-haired front man for a prominent evangelical institution must necessarily be plain vanilla will be in for a jolt. He was never a murderer or a drug addict or a philanderer, but his life holds more than enough with which anyone can identify.

When George Sweeting became the sixth president of the Moody Bible Institute in August 1971, he completed a resonant circle that began late in the nineteenth century when D. L. Moody and Ira Sankey launched evangelistic campaigns in the British Isles in 1873–75, which shook Great Britain to its core.

Moody, already famous in the United States, came to York and began with a small group and what appeared little interest. As curiosity built, he moved on to what became a large crusade in Newcastle, then to Edinburgh, the seat of Scottish Presbyterianism. (George Sweeting is fond of saying that all Scots are Presbyterians unless they've been tampered with. He has also been known to quip that some Scotch Presbyterians are a little heavier on the Scotch than they are on the Presbyterian.)

The Moody/Sankey meetings exploded, and by the time the revival reached Glasgow, ten to twenty thousand people a night gathered in the Botanic Gardens, the only forum large enough to hold the crowds. Within a year after having arrived in Britain, Moody and Sankey were the rage.

When Moody returned to the States, many of the revived Christians returned to the Church of Scotland and found it too formal. They wanted something different. Tent Hall and Bethany Hall were erected in Glasgow, and both became hotbeds of enthusiastic evangelism. Both played a role in George Sweeting's father's life several years later.

Young William Sweeting of Glasgow (born April 2, 1893) was a muscular, blue-eyed and brown-haired man about five-foot ten and 175 pounds. He apprenticed seven years as a third-generation bricklayer before serving three years with the Royal Engineers in Belgium and France during World War I. During his tour of duty he learned he needed salvation but made no decision.

Shortly after his return from service, he lived in Carstairs Junction during the week while building a bridge, visiting his Glasgow home on the weekends. In Carstairs Junction he met a young girl named Mary Rodger Irving, who lived a few hundred feet from the site of the bridge. He was impressed with how easily and forthrightly she talked about her faith, though she was the only Christian in her family. She had been brought to faith in an after-school Bible class in her village, led by a lady named Jesse Kay.

Some time later, William, an accomplished player of the concertina (an instrument akin to a miniature accordion), fell under conviction while playing an old hymn. On his knees, he received Christ. He, like Mary, was the only believer in his family. He began attending Bethany Hall, where he joined with others and played his concertina at open-air meetings at Bridgeton Cross, Glasgow. In the mornings the parishioners fed the needy. In the afternoons they held Bible study meetings. At night they hosted great rallies, inviting the unsaved.

William Sweeting jumped into ministry with both feet. He gave up playing his concertina at dances, and he quit playing semiprofessional soccer because he felt it contributed to his penchant for gambling. He also announced that he was through smoking his pipe. His family was not too sympathetic. His parents chuckled at his profession of faith. His father told him, "I'll hold onto your pipe for you. You'll be wanting it back in a month or two." He never did.

William Sweeting and Mary Irving (born June 21, 1897) were married September 1, 1920. A little more than a year later, Mary gave birth to twins, Bill and Anne. Following the war, finding employment was nearly impossible. William Sweeting was fed up with war and with the fact that Britain seemed to always be involved in a skirmish. He believed the United States was a land of opportunity and a country that would maintain an isolationist military position. He didn't want his son to ever have to go to war.

Following the lead of his uncle on his mother's side, Jack Beattie, William saved his money and set sail for America alone in March 1923.

Not normally an expressive man, William later frequently recounted his thrill at seeing the Statue of Liberty appear on the horizon. For him it was an emotional symbol of a fresh start. That was as close as he would come to weeping as an adult. He once told his children that he was unable to cry.

As he hoped, William Sweeting immediately found work as a bricklayer. He rented a house in Haledon, New Jersey, directly across Kossuth Street from his Uncle Jack, then sent for his wife and twins. They arrived in Boston in October and took a train to Paterson where William picked them up. In that rented home, George Sweeting was born a year later on October 1, 1924. The following May George's father paid $4,900 for a modest home at 103 Church Street, where Anne, Bill, George, and eventually Norman (1928), Mary (1932), and Martha (1935) grew up.

George's Uncle Robert (his father's brother) moved in with the family in 1928 upon his arrival from Scotland and lived with the Sweetings five years. Sister Jean arrived in 1930, so four adults and six children made an otherwise comfortable home crowded for several years. There was only one bathroom, but the elder William Sweeting added three bedrooms in the attic.

George's father was particular about where he worshiped, and after trying a Methodist church in Haledon for a couple of years, he joined Prospect Park Baptist. He was a feisty, overt witness, active in rescue mission work, evangelistic meetings, and music. He taught a Tuesday evening adult Bible class for thirty years. During the 1930s he teamed up with a couple named Clarence and Margie Van Allen, who played violin and Hawaiian guitar. He and his concertina made it a threesome, and the Sweeting/Van Allen Trio played and gave their testimonies in churches and at meetings in the area for many years.

William Sweeting was a strict disciplinarian, not hesitant to occasionally use a razor strap on his sons. His eldest son and namesake was most prone to back talk, so he was the most frequent recipient of the strap. George recalls having done things "just as bad if not worse than Bill" but not suffering as much for it because he kept his mouth shut and didn't argue or sass. The children were told before company arrived that they were to be seen and not heard. If a child was not home in time for supper, he went to bed without, with few exceptions.

William Sweeting was a man of intense principle. He wasn't swayed by what anyone else did or said. If something was right, it was right. If it was wrong, it was wrong. He was forthright and strong willed, and though he was of average size, he feared no man. He was quiet—but not about his faith.

But he wasn't perfect. He brought his prejudices to America. Catholics were anathema to him. His children tried to reason with him, reminding him that in America he didn't have to wage Protestant/Catholic battles. They encouraged him to be civil to a lovely Catholic neighbor family, but he would scarcely speak to them. "They're all mickies [Irish], and they worship the pope."

On the positive side, he instilled in his children the idea that the word *can't* should be eliminated from their vocabularies. "I can do all things through Christ which strengtheneth me," he would say. His biblical mandate was tested to the limit during the Great Depression in the late twenties and thirties. After having done fairly well for himself and his family for almost five years, he lost his job and nearly the house. Building stopped all over the country. If it hadn't been for eleventh-hour financial help from the Van Allens, the house would have been sold. George remembers potential buyers coming through and the whole family praying that they wouldn't like the house. "And if there was something we could do to ensure they didn't like it, we did that, too."

One Christmas during the Depression, Mr. Sweeting waited until the last minute to buy a tree, hoping to find one marked down to fifty cents on Christmas Eve. But he waited too long, wound up with none, and faced a stunned, tearful family the next morning.

The hardest thing William Sweeting ever had to do was to accept relief from the government. It went against his very fiber.

When he couldn't find work as a bricklayer, he took a job as a watchman on the graveyard shift at a silk mill for a fraction of his normal salary. The whole family—parents, children, and even Bob and Jean—were put to work taking in washing and ironing, sewing, making hatbands for a nearby factory, selling rugs and stockings, and making crepe paper flowers and selling them door-to-door. Bill and

George sold Liberty magazines and Radio Guides and, when they were old enough, worked as helpers on a predawn milk route. Ninety percent of their dollar-a-day wage went to the family kitty, and they were expected to tithe a penny from the remaining dime.

Mr. Sweeting bought a shoe mending kit and repaired the family's shoes himself. Mrs. Sweeting sewed most of the children's clothes. She also learned to fill ten hungry stomachs on a small amount of money. Meat was for adults only. Rice, potatoes, beans, and macaroni casseroles were staples for the children. They never ate out.

Mrs. Sweeting let George's blond hair grow long for several years in the European tradition, and he was considered a beautiful baby and young boy. He was a smiler and a cuddler and a tease, and for some reason he was inordinately generous. When the children somehow earned a nickel, they couldn't wait to find something on which to spend it. George took his home and offered to share it with his parents or aunt or uncle. Norman remembers that no matter how little George had, he was always willing to share it with his little brother.

A cynic might surmise that he was trying to buy affection or acceptance from a strong, distant father. Yet this tendency toward generosity apparently began so early and so purely that it seems to have been part of his personality.

George Sweeting was, however, born in sin. Thus another side of his personality was also fully evident during the early years.

2

Halcyon Halcyon Days

*A*ll but the last of William and Mary Sweeting's children were born at home. George remembers when Norman arrived. His mother had been in labor several hours before the doctor was summoned.

Father instructed the children to wait in the living room for what seemed an eternity. Anne and Bill were veterans at age seven. They'd been through this four years before with George, but their experience provided little comfort when the sounds of their mother in pain could not be masked. For George, it was new—and frightening.

Then, suddenly, there were excited voices, a slap, and a wail. Father and the doctor brought the screaming, red baby to the living room. In a few minutes, everyone gathered around Mother's bed. Norman was such a handsome baby that the family began calling him Cutie, a nickname he despises to this day. (George still threatens to have it printed on the back of a sweatshirt for a gift.)

Though both George and Norman say that their brother Bill had as much influence on their lives as anyone, they were close to each other as children and remain so. All three boys became ministers, but the two younger ones recall with admiration the fact that their older brother was—despite his penchant for insisting on the last word with his father—truly the most spiritual as a youngster. In spite of his being three years older than George and seven years older than Norman, he always had time for them, encouraging them, and being the kind of big brother they would have wanted to be.

Bill was not particularly athletic as George and Norm were, so it didn't bother him much when his father forbade high school sports. The younger ones pleaded and begged, but their father equated his sporting days with gambling, smoking, and a bad crowd, so there was no changing his mind.

George recalls that although Bill was somewhat spiritual from the beginning, he and Norm were scrappers. "I had curly blond hair, which made me the butt of constant teasing. But my parents had told us the stories of the Covenanters, Scots who had opposed Roman Catholicism and stood up for their faith. They often said, 'Laddie, you've got the blood of the Covenanters in your veins.' I took that to mean that I should be a fighter. I'm glad my children didn't inherit that tendency."

George fought effectively and often, always trying to prove himself as an outsider—a first-generation American with a European hairstyle. But it was Norm who could handle anyone close to his age and size. "If they were too small for me, I'd sic Norm on them. He could take anybody his size and most anybody bigger and older, too. If one of us wasn't fighting, the other was."

Norm reminisces that George was mostly the arranger and promoter of his fights. "I don't know what that says about him—that he enjoyed having a little brother who was a brawler—but he was constantly egging me on."

As close as they were, they had their own scrapes too. They argued over who was to go get a baby doll carriage one of their younger sisters had left down the street. Mrs. Sweeting had said, "One of you boys go get it."

"You get it, Norm," George said.

"I'm not going to go get it," Norm said. "You go."

Mrs. Sweeting had little patience for such nonsense. "Both of you go get it!"

They trudged down the street, George angry and Norm keeping his distance. Norm knew he was in trouble when George grabbed the carriage and wheeled it around. He ran toward Norm, who didn't have enough time to accelerate. Just as Norm almost reached full speed, the carriage rammed into the back of his leg, digging a deep, blood-spouting gash.

Today it might have required stitches, but in those days it was common for parents to tape up such wounds. Mrs. Sweeting did the work, and Norm recalls that George didn't get into much trouble over it, "because she figured we were both responsible." Norm still sports the scar.

Before she died, Mrs. Sweeting reminisced that she once discovered that George had used an unacceptable method to keep an eye on his little brother. "He had been told to watch Norman, but he wanted to play football or something with his friends. I suppose he decided that the only way he could make sure Norman was safe was to tie him to a nearby tree. Needless to say, that didn't happen twice."

George detested his hair until he was finally allowed to have it trimmed. There were still occasions for scuffles, however. George confronted a bully at school—even though the bully was much bigger. When the bully threatened a boy, George grabbed a baseball bat. "You hit that kid, and I'll split your skull." The bully backed off. "I could have been killed," George says now. "But I did have guts."

Other forms of fun in those days included the children's making their own toys. They played baseball with makeshift equipment. They turned swamp reeds into soft spears. They made a parachute out of an old sheet. They were not wealthy, but they never lacked things to do. Work before play was the law, and there was plenty of time for both.

Mrs. Sweeting was the spiritual heart of the home, a woman of prayer. She had two close friends, Deana Stam and Jessie Cook, who often joined her once a month for a prayer meeting. Deana was the wife of attorney Jacob Stam, who became a member of the board of trustees at Moody, and sister-in-law to John and Betty Stam, who were martyred in China. The Sweeting children often heard those women pray that God would mightily use their children in His service. Two Stam children, two Cook children, and three Sweetings were later called into Christian service.

Young Bill Sweeting would be one of the first answers to those prayers. For much of his youth he was an ideal child—industrious, willing to work, and serious-minded. He led the younger children in playing church. Bill and George took turns leading the singing and preaching. George could imitate any of the radio preachers of the day—and many of the comedians. One of the girls played the piano. The kids used a pie tin for an offering plate, pretended books were hymnals, sang, gave announcements, preached, and prayed. If the iceman or the vegetable peddler or the milkman came by, he would be invited to sit in on the service. It could be said that George Sweeting has been preaching nearly all his life.

On Sunday afternoons the family listened to Percy Crawford and the *Young People's Church of the Air* from Pinebrook, Pennsylvania. George can still imitate Crawford perfectly, as he can Charles Fuller, A. W. Tozer, and Vance Havner.

Radio fascinated the children. The Sweetings allowed them to listen to the tear-jerking innocence of Montana Slim, Hank Snow, and Gene Autry singing country and western tunes every Saturday morning. They were also allowed to listen to *Jack Armstrong: All-American Boy* and *The Lone Ranger* in the afternoons, but otherwise their father strictly regulated their listening. George built himself a tiny crystal radio set with ear phones and fell asleep every Monday night with them on, after having listened to the *Lux Radio Theatre*.

Mr. Sweeting listened to Lowell Thomas every night at seven. In 1972 Lowell Thomas visited the Institute. A warm friendship developed between Dr. Sweeting and Lowell Thomas. A New York station broadcast Big Ben striking twelve in London live every evening, and William Sweeting turned that up loud. It seemed to connect him to Britain, the land he had left for more opportunity and less war.

The Sweeting children had the impression that their mother had always wished their father had been a preacher. The whole family went to hear him play and testify almost every week, and it was during those times that they saw their parents the happiest.

Mrs. Sweeting was a woman who loved to laugh, and she was far more expressive than her husband. A good student and a fair writer, she had, in George's opinion, the soul of a poet. She did whatever she had to to interest the children, from reading them books and poems and Scripture to telling them stories and exhorting them in their faith. Even after they were grown and into the ministry, her sons told her she was the best preacher in the family.

George remembers her as a tireless worker who may have overdone it. Keeping house, cooking, sewing, and attending church kept her going from dawn to midnight nearly every day. Often it was clear that she was run-down, and she was susceptible to illnesses, but no one could slow her. Everyone pitched in and helped, but still there was work to do, and she picked up the slack.

At Thanksgiving and Christmas Mrs. Sweeting worked beyond all limits. She invited friends and family and placed a spread before them that was unrivaled anywhere. For days she baked pies—huge, double tins of mince, lemon meringue, apple, pumpkin, and other kinds. Then, in the cold weather, she still went out to hang her laundry.

It shouldn't have surprised anyone when she was stricken with rheumatoid arthritis. There was little known about the disease, but everyone who knew her assumed she had worn herself to the point where she had no immunity from disease. At times her joints were so painfully inflamed that she couldn't stand to have a sheet over her. William Sweeting designed a special frame that held the sheets over her without touching her. Although the intense pain came and went with her strength and with weather conditions, she suffered with the disease for the rest of her life.

Some believed that if he'd had the money, William would have moved her to a warmer, drier climate. Everyone was sympathetic and pitched in, but she hated being waited upon and having others do her work, so whenever she could she got up and did it herself.

Though his mother was painfully ill for the rest of his childhood,

George recalls that his was a happy, pleasant, noisy home. Neighbors and friends helped out a lot, and one family saw to it that the Sweetings received a huge dinner of finnan haddie, a fish dish, every Friday night. They may have been the only Protestant family in New Jersey that ate fish every Friday. George grew so tired of it that the smell of it nauseates him today.

Uncle Bob Sweeting was an aspiring artist, and it was from watching him that George developed his interest in art. In grade school he loved art class. He also did well in literature and history, but he never cared for math and science. Because of his optimistic good nature, he was popular with both students and teachers—though he was not above reproach. While in the fourth grade he stopped by a swamp on the way to school to pick a bouquet of lilies for his teacher. She was grateful, but he was so filthy from wading into the mucky swamp that she had to send him home to change.

By sixth grade, George was occasionally sent out of class for giggling. Once he began he couldn't stop. It didn't matter what struck his funny bone. He would stifle a laugh till his shoulders shook, his face turned red, and before anyone knew it, guffaw until he had to leave the room.

Usually the admonition was the same. "You stand out in the hall, young man, until you can control yourself." By the time he returned, of course, the source of his amusement had passed. He would tiptoe back to his desk, trying to avoid the smirks of his classmates. But when he sat down, he would burst into laughter and again have to leave the room.

One story George's father never heard concerned George's performance as a Junior Policeman. The Junior Police were precursors to today's crossing guards, and big brother Bill was in charge. He enlisted George, who turned out never to be successful at it. Once he bought a corncob pipe, filled it with tobacco from OPBs (other people's butts), and helped children across the street while smoking. "My father would have killed me," he says.

Above all, William Sweeting wanted his children grounded in the Word of God and immersed in the work ethic. The latter was accomplished with the help of the Sweetings' neighbors across the street, the Whittens. Mr. Whitten owned three milk routes, and over the years he enlisted the Sweeting boys as helpers on the trucks. They couldn't drive until they were seventeen, but in the meantime they ran the milk bottles to and from the doorsteps on all the routes.

George began at age eleven running milk from midnight Friday until eight in the morning. Later, on Saturday, he would cover the route again, delivering double because there was no Sunday run, and collecting money. Though he learned how to handle all the money on the route, he made just a dollar a day. It was hard, demanding, exhausting work. Though he hated the hours, he loved the camaraderie and the sense of independence and accomplishment it gave him. To this day, his memories of the Whitten family are very special.

As for his father's wish that he also become grounded in the Bible, the search for just the right church for the family was to finally end, but not without sacrifice.

3

A Turning Point

eorge cannot point to one moment when he remembers receiving Christ as his Savior. He does not recall ever having not believed. During his childhood he frequently and earnestly "prayed the prayer" when evangelists or pastors urged people. He believed, repented of his sins, and asked Christ to take over his life several times until he learned that it was a once-for-all transaction.

"In my early teens," he says, "I realized that I knew the Lord, and I was His. I memorized verses that assured me, and I would say, 'Lord, You love me; You died for me; I've yielded myself to You. The Bible says that if I believe, I should not perish but have everlasting life [John 3:16b]. So that settles it.'" After that he seldom doubted his salvation, but he experienced rumblings inside that indicated that his spiritual life was not all it should have been.

When George was around twelve, his father decided to leave Prospect Park Baptist Church and try Madison Avenue Baptist in Paterson, a large church with a dynamic Bible-teaching pastor named Edward Drew. Prospect Park appeared to have little concern for evangelism and was dying as far as William Sweeting was concerned. In time it in fact did expire.

The move was good for the adults, and William Sweeting was

greatly challenged by the teaching and preaching. He was troubled, however, because the church appeared to lack a vigorous youth program. His children were getting to the stages where a vibrant approach to the Scriptures was crucial for their development. Madison Avenue Baptist had begun a mission work in Hawthorne called the Hawthorne Gospel Church, and it was reputed to have a solid, self-effacing pastor—Herrmann Braunlin—and a strong youth ministry.

Much as he hated leaving Madison Avenue Baptist and Pastor Drew, William Sweeting decided that he must leave for the sake of his children. It meant a longer drive every Sunday, but in January of 1938, when George Sweeting was thirteen years old, Hawthorne Gospel became his family's home church. Amazingly, Herrmann Braunlin would pastor that church for sixty-two years before retiring in the 1980s. George Sweeting would not only solidify his relationship to Christ in that church, but he would also be baptized, meet his wife, get married, become ordained, and return to accept an associate pastor's role.

By the late thirties the Depression was lifting. The building trades were some of the first to call their workers back. When William Sweeting began working again the economic burden lightened. The immigrants, however, who had come to America for opportunity and had tasted it, were humiliated by the Depression. In one sense they never recovered. They never again could live in confidence that their families, their jobs, their incomes would be secure. Life would not be the same for them again.

Like the rest, William and Mary Sweeting became wary, cautious, frugal. There were no guarantees in life, no promised lands this side of heaven. The family still rarely went out to eat—that was for the comfortably wealthy. Vacations were unheard of. Mr. Sweeting might take the family to the ocean on Saturday, his day off, but it was a one-day trip. They never stayed overnight in a hotel.

Even when William Sweeting rose to the level of foreman, he didn't relax and enjoy his position. He was tough, a hard driver, a confronter. When he overheard foul language, he challenged the culprit, "Does this look like a sewer? I'm not working in a garbage dump, so what makes you think I want to hear any of your garbage?"

No one loafed under him, and his projects were done ahead of schedule.

He loved to say that one of his men once reminded him, "Scottie, Rome wasn't built in a day."

"I told him, 'That's 'cause I wasn't the foreman on that job!'"

When the Sweetings finally got their first telephone, it was for emergencies only. It hardly ever rang, and when it did, it was cause for alarm. Chatting on the phone was forbidden.

After he had become a foreman and even began teaching evenings in a local vocational school, William Sweeting allowed himself one luxury. The daily paper was delivered to the house. If the children read it before he did, they had to put it back exactly as they found it. After the evening meal and the daily, family devotional he led, the kids went off to do chores or play ball, and he headed to his corner to read his paper. That was his inviolate daily regimen for years.

The daily devotions fit the church-centered family life, and the only thing that would interrupt them was if the children got the giggles. Mr. Sweeting would tolerate that only so far and then he would become upset. Otherwise he had the joy of the Lord, and his favorite theme was the return of Christ. One of George's most vivid memories is of the time his father read of the second coming and asked them individually, "Bill, if Christ comes tonight, are you ready? Anne, are you ready? George, are you ready? Norman, are you ready? Mary, are you ready? Martha, are you ready?" When all assured him they were ready, the family sang, "Will the Circle Be Unbroken?"

Mr. and Mrs. Sweeting were not given to overt praise of their children. If there was anything Mary Sweeting felt as strongly as that there was no higher calling than the ministry, it was that a person should not be unduly honored. To protect against that, she and her husband rarely honored their children—even when honor was due. George cannot remember being complimented by his father. As he progressed in life to become a student leader, then an evangelist and chalk artist, a pastor, and a well-known evangelical, his parents rarely came to hear him speak unless he was in his hometown—and sometimes not even then. When they did come, he had to determine their reaction from the expressions on their faces.

Even if other people tried to encourage their children by praising one of their accomplishments, it bothered them. "They were afraid I'd get bigheaded, and the Scots can't stand anyone who thinks he's hot stuff."

At fourteen, George asked his father's permission to buy a bicycle. "Sure. You pay for it, you can have it." It was a skeptical challenge, but George was determined. A brand-new bike was thirteen dollars, which meant that by saving his nine cents a week for three years, he could afford one. He found ways to supplement that meager income, but still the going was slow. His only extravagance during that period were root beer barrels, hard candy that sold two for a penny. He still buys a couple when he can find them.

George was the hit of the family and of the neighborhood when he finally came home with that bike. He beamed, and he detected a twinkle of pride in his father's eyes, too, but Mr. Sweeting said nothing.

During those years Pastor Braunlin brought speakers in every summer for several weeks of nightly meetings at the Summer Pavilion on Lafayette Avenue, property owned by the Hawthorne Gospel Church. The best-known evangelists, pastors, educators, and musicians were invited in for a few days or a week at a time from June through September. A meeting was held at 7:45 nightly, and three times on Sunday. It may have been one of the most ambitious yearly Bible conference programs in the United States. Regardless where those great speakers went in the rest of the country, when they made the swing to the East Coast, they headed for Hawthorne Gospel's Summer Pavilion.

The Sweeting family tried to make it out to many of the meetings each week. George was fascinated by what he heard and saw. Will H. Houghton, president of the Moody Bible Institute, spoke, as did Dr. Walter L. Wilson, Porter Barrington, and chalk artists Phil Saint and P. H. Kadey. It was while seeing Saint and Kadey that George decided he could have a similar ministry. He built an easel in the garage and practiced day after day, painting, drawing, mimicking what he had seen. In his mind he had found his future. He wanted to be an artist. That was his goal, and he was sure he was going to be one.

The Hawthorne Gospel Church answered William Sweeting's prayer beyond his wildest dreams. His children were involved in three to four services every Sunday from Sunday school to morning church to youth group, and evening church. The high school youth group had no frills, no skits, no games, no fooling around. They had their fun at socials, but the lessons were taken seriously.

Pastor Braunlin and laymen led teams of the young people through the Bible, verse by verse, and they covered every doctrine over a period of years. But these teams were not there to simply drink it in; their task was to master the material each week so that they could teach it to the rest of the young people. The teams were made up of only those who were serious about their walks of faith.

That young people's group was the tail that wagged the church. George's older brother, Bill, was one of the more devout, teaching a Bible class that George occasionally attended at the high school. A group called the Inspiration Messengers taught and preached and sang and played at hospitals, nursing homes, rescue missions, and small rural churches. The kids gained experience ministering in a variety of ways to audiences of every age and type, as well as learning to be spiritually sensitive to each other.

George's Sunday school class was similar. He studied under a layman named Johnny Roe in a class of about a hundred boys. Johnny had a grade school education, but he was organized. He had every boy's name in a loose-leaf notebook. He prayed for each and kept track of their progress in ministry. He prayed about each assignment and then announced it. "George, I feel that you should speak this week."

"Johnny, I can't preach. Let me lead the singing again."

"You preach. Just give 'em your testimony. Tell 'em what Jesus did for you."

The boys went to rescue missions, jails, hospitals, anywhere

Johnny could arrange for them to minister. Even though George hadn't committed himself wholeheartedly to serving the Lord yet, he was getting invaluable training. It was Johnny Roe who got him started doing chalk drawings while he preached. John Van Der Eerus and Barney Van Dyke also continually encouraged George to prepare for Christian Service.

Late in 1939, during his sophomore year in high school and shortly after he turned fifteen, George noticed a new girl in the youth group. Her name was Hilda Schnell. Her father ran a bakery in Fairlawn and had switched from the Brethren Assembly in Paterson for the same reason William Sweeting had moved his family to Hawthorne Gospel: the youth program. Even though the Schnells were immigrants to the United States from Germany and would have been much more comfortable staying in the German services at the Assembly, they were more concerned with the spiritual welfare of their children.

Hilda, then thirteen, was taken with George's sense of humor and smile. She thought he was cute and was impressed that he seemed so popular with the rest of the young people.

They didn't date each other for more than a year, but they saw each other at church and youth group and were in the Inspiration Messengers together. Things didn't really click between them until George made sure he was on the same toboggan with her at a social the following winter, and he likes to say they're still on it.

But a lot was to happen in young George's life between the time he first saw Hilda Schnell and when he fell in love with her. His life revolved around the church and the youth group. Although he wasn't a rebel or a troublemaker, and he was far from a scoffer, he still was not totally sold out to Christ.

That changed when he and Hilda and several others from the youth group attended a revival in Paterson preached by evangelist George T. Stevens. George Sweeting worked as a counselor at the meetings and led his first convert to Christ. He was drawn to a deeper walk with God through the experience and didn't miss one night of the forty-one-day crusade. He still thought he would grow up to become an artist, but he knew it was time to get serious about his faith.

He threw himself into the public ministries of the youth group with new vigor. He meant business with God and wanted to serve Him even though he didn't know there was yet another step along his spiritual path before he found his niche.

4

Appointment at the Pavilion

The most memorable night of George Sweeting's life was Friday, August 16, 1940. It was the summer before his junior year in high school, and he was six weeks from his sixteenth birthday. He had tried to make the Friday and Sunday meetings at the Pavilion all summer, and this Friday broke hot under a cloudless sky. The night sky was still light, and there was not even a hint of a breeze when the meeting started. The crowd was average for David Otis Fuller, pastor of the Wealthy Street Baptist Church in Grand Rapids, Michigan. He had spoken nightly since Monday.

As the music and offering and other preliminaries ended, the sun began to set and the paper fans fell idle. A light, warm breeze wafted through the Pavilion, and Pastor Fuller was introduced to speak. George can't specifically remember one word preached. All he knows is that Fuller was a direct man, zinging challenges at the audience, willing them to listen, to decide. What would it be? in or out? saved or not? consecrated or not? real or not? a dynamic faith or a false faith?

George was normally a politely attentive listener. He could relax, let his mind wander, think of a joke, make sketches, take notes, write notes, depending on what was going on around him. But this night his attention was riveted to the platform. He hardly moved. Not only was David Otis Fuller speaking to him, so was God. The crux of the message was James 1:22, about not only being hearers of the Word but doers also.

Deep in his heart and mind he realized he had failed to obey the truths he claimed to believe. He sensed that God wanted all of him, everything, no holding back. It meant no saying you mean business and then still trying to determine for yourself what your future held, what you should be, where you should go. The young people around him might have been chatting, giggling, and squirming. He doesn't know. One or two might have even nudged him, whispered his name, or tried to get his attention. He was in his own world, a world small enough for him and big enough for God.

Fuller went long. The sun died, and the cloudless, black sky sparkled with stars. Women pulled sweaters around their shoulders, and men slipped on jackets. George Sweeting just sat staring, listening to Fuller, open to God. He felt emotion welling up within. That was not like him. He had been humorous but not emotional, like his parents. Scots. Stoics. Yet the tears pushed to the brims of his eyes. His fists were clenched. God was speaking to him. He wanted to hear it all, get it straight, commit himself once and for all, for now and forever, no matter what it meant, no matter what the cost.

No one responded as the crowd stood to sing. George couldn't sing. It was all he could do to stand. An invitation was given to those Christians who wanted to rededicate their lives, but somehow that didn't fit him, either. He sensed God calling him not to repentance or rededication or to any public statement or witness. He felt an urging of the Lord to a private decision, a stepping over the line, a definite call to full-time service.

The meeting ended, and people began milling about. His friends made their plans for a burger and a Coke at the diner as usual. Who would ride with whom? Are you going? Can you take me home? George, are you coming? He shook his head. "Not tonight, thanks." Often the life of the party, he was grateful no one challenged him, pushed him, insisted to know why not. He made his way down to

Pastor Braunlin as the place slowly emptied. Finally, the tears flowed. The pastor could see that George had been moved. He sat with him in the front row and waited for George to speak. "Pastor," he began, "the Lord spoke powerfully to me tonight. I'm yielding my life to Christ. I know the verses, but I want to put them into practice. I've been a halfhearted Christian, but I feel a call to His service. From now on, I'm going to be all out. I will serve Christ anywhere, anytime."

Herrmann Braunlin was never the type to get too excited. He was a warm, loving, methodical man, given to doing what was right because it was right. He took the news calmly but was obviously pleased. Just above a whisper, he said, "George, that's good. That's exactly what you should do. Can I reread tonight's Scripture passage to you?" George nodded and the pastor opened his well-worn Bible to James 1 and read verses 5 through 22:

If any of you lack wisdom, let him ask of God, that giveth to all men liberally, and upbraideth not; and it shall be given him.

But let him ask in faith, nothing wavering. For he that wavereth is like a wave of the sea driven with the wind and tossed.

For let not that man think that he shall receive any thing of the Lord.

A doubleminded man is unstable in all his ways.

Let the brother of low degree rejoice in that he is exalted:

But the rich, in that he is made low: because as the flower of the grass he shall pass away.

For the sun is no sooner risen with a burning heat, but it withereth the grass, and the flower thereof falleth, and the grace of the fashion of it perisheth: so also shall the rich man fade away in his ways.

Blessed is the man that endureth temptation: for when he is tried, he shall receive the crown of life, which the Lord hath promised to them that love him.

Let no man say when he is tempted, I am tempted of God: for God cannot be tempted with evil, neither tempteth he any man:

But every man is tempted, when he is drawn away of his own lust, and enticed.

Then when lust hath conceived, it bringeth forth sin: and sin, when it is finished, bringeth forth death.

Do not err, my beloved brethren.

Every good gift and every perfect gift is from above, and cometh down from the Father of lights, with whom is no variableness, neither shadow of turning.

Of his own will begat he us with the word of truth, that we should be a kind of firstfruits of his creatures.

Wherefore, my beloved brethren, let every man be swift to hear, slow to speak, slow to wrath:

For the wrath of man worketh not the righteousness of God. Wherefore lay apart all filthiness and superfluity of naughtiness, and receive with meekness the engrafted word, which is able to save your souls.

But be ye doers of the word, and not hearers only, deceiving your own selves.

The place was nearly empty when Pastor Braunlin looked up from his Bible. George could see his own glow mirrored on the man's face. Without a word the pastor knelt. George knelt with him. The man who would, in essence, be George Sweeting's pastor his whole life, prayed a simple prayer, committing him to the will of God.

It was late. To get home, George normally took a ten-mile bus ride into Paterson and then a nearly three-mile bus ride to Haledon. George didn't mind the ride that night. He couldn't keep from smiling. He'd held nothing back. Finally, at long last, he belonged completely and irrevocably to God for whatever He wanted. When the bus stopped in Paterson, he got off and walked the rest of the way. Any other night it would have been wearying, but he says he felt as if one foot hit the pavement, saying, "Hallelujah," and the other hit, saying, "Praise the Lord."

"I floated home," he says.

Mrs. Sweeting was a woman who didn't go to bed until all her children were home. It was her custom to sit on the front porch and greet each one as they returned, asking them about their evenings.

George found her sitting there with the newspaper over her for warmth against what had become a chilly breeze. As soon as she saw him, she knew. "Son, God did something special for you tonight, didn't He?"

George eagerly told her all the details. His mother, who had always told him that "we Scots don't wear our feelings on our sleeves," was now nearly overcome. "Your father and I dedicated you to the Lord before you were born," she said. "If God calls you to preach, don't shrink and become a king or a president!" The Sweetings had always said they believed there was no higher calling in the world than the ministry. "What an honor," she now added in her thick brogue, "to be able to preach the Word of God and to tell others the way of salvation."

They talked for nearly an hour about the will and the timing of God and how He works in mysterious ways. She told George of her own walk with God over the years and how He had proved faithful in every detail, in spite of her suffering and hardship. Then, for the second time that night, George was invited to kneel and join in prayer. His mother committed him to Christ and prayed that he would never waver from his resolve. Before he went to his room she asked him, "What do I always say about God?"

George smiled and quoted her, "He is too good to be unkind and too wise to make a mistake."

By the time he reached his attic bedroom he was ready to pray again. He didn't want the night to end or the feeling to leave him. Every step on the way home had given him the opportunity to vow before God that he had soberly thought it through and was firm and unflinching. Now he felt led to put his lifetime goals on paper, specifically in the flyleaf of his Scofield Bible.

He knelt by his bed and wrote:

1. *I want to seek, above everything else, to bring glory to God (1 Corinthians 10:31).*

2. *I will strive to cultivate the inner life (2 Peter 3:18).*

3. *I will disciple as many people as humanly possible (Matthew 28:19–20).*

4. By God's grace I'll win as many to Christ as humanly possible (Proverbs 11:30).

George was never the same. He felt imbued with a power that could come only from the Holy Spirit. All he wanted to do was to tell other people about Jesus Christ. He accepted every assignment to teach, to give a testimony, to lead singing, to preach, to draw. As a teenager he preached somewhere just about every week. He says he felt he would have rather preached than eat, and he often did.

His brother Bill had left home to attend Mr. Moody's school, as his parents had always called it, and it wasn't long before George began hearing from Bill what a wonderful place it was to learn and grow and serve and fellowship with other believers.

George set his sights on attending Moody in two years. His father told him, "I can't give you a dime, but I'll pray for you every day."

George became a bold, overt, but not offensive, testimony at Central High School. Over the course of his last two years, he would see dozens come to know Christ as a result of his witness, forty-one during his senior year alone.

Meanwhile, winter came, including the youth group's toboggan social where things seemed to click with Hilda Schnell. She was a trim, pretty girl with a soft-spoken, shy manner that still describes her. George's public gifts and ease with people were a perfect balance for her, and she delighted in quietly watching him speak. What many didn't realize, and still don't, was that the closer they grew, the more important to him became her deeply spiritual influence. She was and is a wise counselor, a woman of the Word and of prayer.

George and Hilda became an item around the church and within the youth group, but they didn't have their first official date, alone together, until the following year. The relationship was cultivated, in part, through chocolate milk and raisin squares. The Schnell Bakery was not on George's milk route—on which he now worked six nights a week from midnight to eight—but his truck rolled past there anyway. It was no problem getting the driver to stop and let George leave the Schnells a bottle of chocolate milk, because he would always come back to the truck with some fresh-baked goodies like eclairs or apple or raisin squares for himself and the driver. When George turned seventeen and was allowed to drive the milk truck himself, the stop at the bakery was automatic.

Once George and Hilda started dating, they spent hours telling each other about themselves. George devoted himself to getting to know the girl he assumed would be his lifelong partner. Though her family was from Germany, their backgrounds were strikingly similar. And although it would be more than a year before she was as sure of her feelings for George as he was of his for her, neither had ever dated anyone else, and they never would.

It wasn't that no one else wanted to date them. In fact, because of his youth and naïveté, a woman ten years George's senior was about to scare him to death with her advances.

5

Roadblocks

The woman, in her mid-twenties, was dynamic and attractive. To George, of course, even though she was a knockout, she was totally off-limits. He had never even thought of her in a romantic way because she was so much older and because he knew her only as one of the youth group sponsors.

He had no reason to assume anything other than that she was a godly woman. Her advice had benefited many of the young women and some of the young men, spurring them to become totally sold-out to God. Everyone knew she had been the innocent victim of a painful divorce, but that had been some years ago, and she had been serving in the church for several years.

George got a hint that everything wasn't as it seemed whenever he spoke about Hilda—which was, of course, frequently. This woman either acted as if she hadn't heard him or looked bored, even troubled. Clearly she didn't care for his affection for Hilda—which he couldn't believe—or she wasn't happy about George's interest in Hilda—which he couldn't understand.

The woman regularly found reasons to talk with George about spiritual things, and then she began making sure he was the last one she dropped off after meetings. Sometimes she wanted to discuss her problems and needs with him, always starting with the spiritual. That threw him off. Other times she asked him to pray with her about her loneliness. When he did, she thanked him with an affectionate touch.

When she drove to a secluded spot for their next discussion and prayer meeting, George finally caught on. He mentioned it to a worldly driver he worked with on the milk run, and the man immediately said, "I know exactly what she wants and needs. Let me meet her."

"No," George insisted, "she's a good woman. A godly woman. I just don't understand it."

"I understand fully," the driver said. "I've heard enough."

Finally George confided his concern to a friend, the son of a deacon. The boy told his father, and the deacons came to George for more details. They had had a similar problem with her and another young man a few years earlier, but nothing serious was ever suspected or charged, and the young man had eventually left the area. A deacon phoned him. God had been speaking to him, and he confessed that the woman had, in fact, seduced him.

The woman was called before the church board and removed from her responsibilities. She left the church, and George never saw her again. That was many years ago, yet it was traumatic, disillusioning, and scary. He still breathes a sigh of relief at his own naiveté and a prayer of thanks for protection against an attack that could have ruined his future usefulness.

Because of Hilda's quiet spirituality and George's still relatively recent calling to Christian service, their early courtship remained on a spiritual plane, even while he was falling for her. Often a romance can dim the light of a first love of Christ following salvation, rededication, or a spiritual calling, but George was determined to follow through on his lifetime goals and covenants. Thus, he was careful to study the woman who captivated him to be certain she would be comfortable with his level of commitment to Christ.

The more he learned about her, the better he felt about the relationship. And although she was shy and reticent and not about to commit herself too soon, he became convinced that God wanted them together. He rested with patience in the confidence her feelings for him would eventually come around. Hilda was the youngest of three girls, and they, like the Sweetings, had learned a work ethic from the beginning. She remembers that when she was about five or six, and her sisters were in their early teens, they all worked for their father in the bakery. Even as a child, she did odd jobs—sweeping, wrapping, boxing, icing. As she grew older, she was taught to work the counter and cash register. She enjoyed selling. On occasion, when a baker didn't show up during the night, Mr. Schnell roused his entire family at 4:00 A.M., informing them that they had to help ice the cakes and finish the cookies and sweet rolls by 6:00 when the bakery opened.

With the outbreak of World War II, her family was persecuted slightly. Her father tried to keep his American political views private so as not to offend a whole faction of customers, but whenever he felt it necessary, he took a stand against Nazism. He and his wife were avid Christians, faithful to the Brethren Assembly until switching to Hawthorne Gospel when Hilda became a teen. When she was little they sometimes hosted Bible studies or prayer meetings in their home, and there were those who spread rumors that Mr. Schnell was a Nazi. Once a stone came through the window during a meeting, but no one was hurt, and the deed was traced to a disturbed neighbor. The rumors bothered Mr. Schnell, because he was far from a Nazi. People gradually developed faith in him because he proved to be an honest, hardworking businessman.

Hilda suspected that her father always had a secret desire that one of his future sons-in-law or grandsons would go into the business with him, as he had no sons of his own. It never happened.

As for what he and his wife expected from his daughters, "First and foremost," he often told them, "we want you to do what the Lord wants you to do."

George Sweeting understood this type of family, and he fell hard for that youngest daughter. "It took her a while to decide," he says, "but I knew from the beginning and never wavered. I never considered anyone else." He and Hilda used to walk in Gofflebrook Park, which ran the length of Hawthorne, and stand on a rustic bridge gazing at the stars and dreaming of what God might have in store for them. Those walks always followed church functions because even at George's age, as a seventeen-year-old senior in high school, the rule was that he had to be in at dark when the streetlights came on unless he was at a church meeting. Regardless of what time he got in, he had to be ready to go out again by eleven or midnight for the milk route.

Driving was much easier than being the helper. As a helper, for years he'd had to run the milk up several flights of stairs—he could carry three quarts in one hand, step over drunks in alleys, run the risk of falling off the running board of the truck while trying to avoid interrupting amorous couples in parked cars, and even watch out for critters. Once he put a bottle of milk on a stoop and saw a skunk lift its tail. He slowly backed away, and the skunk didn't follow through. More than once he beat off an attacking dog with a full bottle of milk.

The hours weren't any better when he became a driver, but the work was more enjoyable. He tried to get home in time to get in an hour or two of sleep before school, but his mother frequently found him difficult to rouse. One morning she called to him, and he came downstairs, still asleep, pulling on his clothes inside out.

One morning at about 1:00 A.M., George parked next to a store on Tenth Street in Paterson, N.J., so that his helper could run a quart up to the third floor of an apartment building. Just before the helper left the truck, however, George checked his book. "Forget it. They're on vacation." The helper stayed on the running board and George pulled away, only to see an army transport truck come barreling down the avenue, out of control. It blasted over the curb, right where he had been parked only seconds before, and smashed through the plate glass window of the store, injuring all three occupants of the truck.

George and his helper pulled them out and called an ambulance. After the soldiers were on their way to the hospital, George and his helper stopped at the next corner. Their knees were like jelly. George believed the Lord had allowed the incident to show him that he was not his own, that he had a higher call, that there was a purpose to his life. His helper was so shaken he was almost in tears.

It gave George the opening to talk about what might have happened to each of them if that truck had hit them. His helper seemed receptive, so George walked him through the tract *Four Things God Wants You to Know*. The man knelt by the running board to receive Christ.

George waited eagerly to hear from Moody after he sent in his application during his senior year of high school. He busied himself with the presidency of the youth group, his milk route, his relationship with Hilda, his involvement as art editor of the school yearbook, and various art projects (including painting the sets for school plays). He still bears a tiny, unintended tattoo on one hand that was caused by his fall from a ladder onto the stage. He hit the floor and his India ink pen hit his hand, embedding beneath the skin a small quantity of ink that remains fifty years later.

When his acceptance from Moody finally arrived, he excitedly shared it with his friends and family, but that was balanced by cold reality. He had little money, and he had never slept anywhere but in his own bed. Never. He had never gone to camp, never stayed in a hotel, never visited relatives or even a buddy overnight. It simply wasn't done in his family. Every single night for more than seventeen years he had slept in his own bed in his own home. Now he faced the prospect of moving out. Fortunately, his brother Bill agreed to be his roommate at Moody.

Now all George had to do was to get through his tough math and chemistry classes, receive his diploma, and try to earn a little more money over the summer. Surprisingly, getting out of high school proved harder than he expected. George shouldn't have been surprised at the difficulties, however, because he brought them on himself.

After having been so active and so evangelistic, it seemed the ultimate coup was getting his own pastor to give the benediction at the graduation exercises. The only problem was that Pastor Braunlin was invited and George Sweeting wasn't.

The trouble was in chemistry, which George detested. The ordeal may have begun with a caricature of the teacher he drew on the board. She was round faced with heavy eyelids and puckered lips, so George cartooned a bucktoothed frog and labeled it with her name. The class howled and so did he until he saw her in the doorway. That didn't resonate with her, and his grades didn't help much, either.

Then there was his plan. Right after lunch was seventh period, during which he had no class. Chemistry was eighth period. If he left at lunchtime, he could walk the two miles to Eastside High and visit Hilda. The problem was that twenty-two times during the final semester he didn't get back to Central in time for eighth period. The teacher failed him with a sixty-nine. He had to take chemistry in summer school to get his diploma.

His parents were shattered when it came to light, and George was humiliated. He told his pastor he knew he'd been wrong and that he was sure it would make him a better student in college. "Tell the Lord about it," Pastor Braunlin advised. "He'll understand and forgive you, even if your parents may not. In five years you'll look back on this and laugh about it."

In truth, he was laughing about it sooner, but it was decades before he told anyone but family about it. In fact, even his sons didn't know about it until recent years, and that was only because his brother Norman advised him to tell them so they wouldn't find him such an impossible act to follow.

George wasn't just blowing smoke when he told his pastor that the experience might make him a better student in the future. He told himself he would be much more serious-minded than ever, once he was on campus at Moody. He would still have fun and enjoy a good prank, a joke, or a laugh. But he wouldn't trifle with his studies.

The thought of leaving home for Moody was bittersweet. He sensed that God had some wonderful opportunities in store for him, even though he wasn't sure what they were. He would have to travel alone because freshmen had to arrive earlier than seniors. Bill gave him instructions on where to get a taxi, what to say, how to get to the school, and a few things to watch out for. Mostly, George worried about how he would do away from the rest of the family, his church friends, and—of course—Hilda.

Would she still be there waiting for him? Would she write daily as she'd promised? The prospect of a tri-semester program that covered eleven months in a year was almost more than he could fathom. He might have been able to handle a standard situation where he had a three-month summer break to look forward to, but not this!

For the next two school years, he would see Hilda only a month during each year. Then he hoped he could talk her into enrolling at Moody for his last year. As it would turn out, absence from his loved ones would prove the least of his problems.

6

On to Moody

When his parents and Hilda saw George off at the Newark station of the Pennsylvania Railroad, he was excited. What an opportunity! Many, many young people from his church had attended Moody, and he had heard about the place from his older brother. His parents had not encouraged him to go to college—in fact, they didn't encourage any of the kids to go because they were unable to help them financially. But still he knew they were pleased. And if you were going to study the Bible, "Mr. Moody's school" was the only place to go. As the Trailblazer began its more than eighteen-hour journey west toward Chicago, George's anxiety rolled with it. At various stops he had to give up his seat to a woman or a child or a serviceman and sit in the aisle on his suitcase. He tried to sleep, but he was too excited. He'd had many opportunities to draw and preach in his home area, and now he was going where he was unknown. He was anxious about Chicago, making his way through the great train station, finding a cab, getting to the Institute. What would it look like? Would the food be good? Would he find new friends? He felt like a nobody from nowhere, and he already missed his family and friends, especially Hilda.

Arriving in Chicago made him feel like a country bumpkin. He wouldn't have known how to get a porter to help him get his bags to a cab, so he just loaded everything on his shoulders and tottered through the terminal, eyes agog over the crushing crowd and the high ceilings. Brother Bill had told him to follow the signs to the street where he would find the taxicabs.

He had never ridden in a cab before, didn't know the protocol of which one to choose, and followed the stream of people heading out one door. He staggered under the weight of his suitcase and 150-pound artist easel. As he'd heard it would be, Chicago was hot, humid, muggy. He didn't have a free hand to wipe his brow.

Right in front of the door was a cab with the driver sitting behind the wheel, reading a newspaper. George moved toward him and stood where he knew the man had to be able to see him in his peripheral vision. He didn't budge. What was a person supposed to say to a cabby?

"Are you working?"

"Are you available?"

"Can I get in?"

"Do you know the way to Moody?"

George didn't know where to start, what to say. Bill had told him to pretend he'd done this a dozen times. Just say the name of the place and the address as if he and everyone in Chicago knew where it was. That way the cabby wouldn't be tempted to run you to Moody via the West Side.

"Sir?" George managed weakly. The driver turned slowly and looked at him. "Can I get a ride?" The driver pursed his lips as if that was the stupidest request he'd heard in a week and jabbed a thumb ahead of him. George looked ahead and realized that this cab was in a bumper-to-bumper line of cabs that extended all the way up the block. Even if he'd got in, his cab would have had to wait until a dozen others had pulled away.

Red-faced, George trudged up the street, only to have to stand in line for his turn at a cab. He didn't want to put his bags down because he'd heard of people who teamed up to distract you while a buddy walked off with your luggage. While he hesitated, people stepped in front of him to take cabs. He knew he would have to act. As one cab pulled away, he strode to the next one. To his surprise the cabby stepped out and helped him load his stuff in the trunk. "Thank you!" No response. "Hot day, huh?" he added as he opened the front door.

"Backseat, pal," the cabby said.

"Oh, sorry."

"Where to?"

"Moody Bible Institute. Eight-twenty North LaSalle." He was tempted to ask if the cabby knew where that was, and he knew he had in no way hidden that he was a first timer to Chicago. The silence was awkward, but he figured that if the driver wanted to he would have said something. "It's near the corner of Chicago Avenue," George added, but the driver barely turned his head. He was already at Wells and Chicago and whipped north and took two rights to let George off in front of the arch.

George tried to remember what the fare was supposed to have been and how much tip to add. He tried to pay while the cabby was helping with his bags, but that wouldn't have worked. Finally, the fare was paid, the cab roared off, and George stood there on LaSalle next to his stuff, gaping at Crowell Hall.

Other people were milling about, but they looked as new and as lost as he felt. There was no welcoming committee and few signs until he got into the arch. Then he just lugged his stuff until he found a long line waiting for freshman registration. He was hot, tired, homesick, and wondering what he had got himself into.

Ahead of him and soon behind him in line were more freshmen. He tried to look self-assured and noticed them trying to do the same. Their introductions and small talk were strained. Everyone was pre-occupied. It was enough to be trying to arrange your payments, your work schedule, and your classes without having to stand there wondering if you had made the right decision about coming in the first place. Homesickness swept over him in waves.

Finally he was given his class schedule and his work assignment. The pittance he had saved up and a small gift from his church had given him just enough to get started. He would have to work at the school and somewhere on his own to make ends meet. With a short stack of linens to add to his burden, he found his way up to his and Bill's room. The skeleton key worked on the third try, and he dragged everything across the threshold and slumped onto the bare-mattressed bed. He sat with his head in his hands. "Lord, help me."

By the time he was unpacked, sent a telegram to Hilda to let her know he had arrived safely (a practice he still continues, no matter where he goes), and went exploring, he started to feel better. A lot of the new students were the children of pastors or evangelists whose names he recognized. That made him feel even more isolated, but he sensed that opportunities to preach and minister would come.

Things were a whole lot better when his brother Bill arrived and classes started. George decided to be conscientious, even in classes he didn't like or found difficult. On one occasion he tried to talk his big brother out of hiding in the closet during a fire drill. "What if it's real, and they find your bones smoking in there?"

During the 1942–43 school year, when he wasn't working just to sustain himself and pay his school bills, George busied himself getting to know as many students and faculty members as he could, studying, writing to Hilda, and handling his PCW (Practical Christian Work) assignments. These were the joy of his life. He not only preached in the jails and rescue missions and taught some Sunday school classes, but he also volunteered to substitute for anyone else's preaching assignments. Frequently there were PCW teams who were strong in every category except preaching. If they had a special meeting, they asked George to come with them.

On special occasions, he toted his 150 pounds worth of easel, lights, and chalk drawing equipment to points all over the Midwest. On those assignments he was usually alone. He frequently didn't return to the Institute until 1:00 or 2:00 in the morning and had to get permission to be out so late. But his fears of not having enough opportunities to preach had vanished. Not only was he preaching just about everywhere in the Midwest, but he was also in demand, unable to fulfill all the requests. He learned the best way he knew how: he took what he heard in class and preached it the next week.

The only snag in his busy schedule was that he had to work so much. He alternated between handling the silverware in the kitchen, mopping Crowell Hall, and serving as a doorman at Jacques, a French restaurant on Delaware Street. He wore a snappy uniform and earned fifty cents an hour, two meals a day, and sometimes as much as ten or fifteen dollars a night in tips. He was a good doorman, and they were patient with him. He seemed to quit every few months because he had saved enough to pay his bills and wanted to devote himself to study and to preaching.

He made a game of remembering where he parked people's cars so that when he saw them coming he could race down the street, find the car, and have it back to them by the time they reached the curb. People appreciated such service and tipped generously, usually in proportion to their level of inebriation.

George grew so weary of answering the question, "So, why aren't you in the army?" he vowed to a friend that he was going to yield to temptation and answer, "For the same reason you aren't in the movies, lady."

But he never did. His mischievous streak did overcome him one night, however, when a couple popped the standard question. "You cut a striking figure in that uniform, young man. Why aren't you in the service?"

"Peg leg," he said sadly, and hobbled off as they tried profusely to apologize. When he returned with their car, he didn't have the heart to come clean, so he just limped out and tipped his cap. It resulted in the largest tip he ever got at Jacques.

Also during his freshman year, George accepted a part-time job as an artist with the nearby Christian film company, Baptista Films. They put him in charge of doing the backgrounds for their films. He hung wallpaper, procured pictures, and did whatever was necessary.

During one series of six films with the late physician and Bible teacher Walter Wilson of Kansas City, George was pressed into duty as a fresh young face who sat and asked the good doctor enough questions to make it look like a conversation. He was not given a script but was prompted to say things such as:

"Yes, Dr. Wilson."

"And then what should I do, Dr. Wilson?"

"Yes, Doctor."

"And then what, Dr. Wilson?"

George and Hilda wrote each other every day during his first two years at Moody. On paper, Hilda felt freer to be more expressive. She was able to return his messages of love. During the brief month between semesters from August to September, he and Hilda had hoped to have some time together. But soon his calendar filled with speaking engagements, and one school year seemed to blend in with the next. It seemed inconceivable that he would find the time to be a doorman, work at the Institute, work at Baptista Films, preach several nights a week, every Friday and Saturday, and at least twice on Sunday.

Once he confided in a classmate that he felt the Lord was going to continue providing him unique opportunities to minister. In his heart he knew he was not getting the big head. He knew who he was and who he wasn't, and he was grateful to God for every gift and every opportunity. But his classmate didn't see it that way. "I guess we all think that about ourselves," he muttered, throwing a wet blanket on George's enthusiasm. But privately George really believed that significant things were in store, and he was thankful to be in the place of usefulness.

George had a hard time saying no. When he realized the opportunities available to him in a big city to improve on his artistic ability, he got permission to enroll in the Art Academy three nights a week. Then he switched over to the Art Institute. George was busy from before dawn until well after midnight, getting by on five hours' sleep, but still making time for personal devotions and for writing Hilda every day.

It was the busiest, most actively hectic time of his life, trying to juggle a ton of assignments, responsibilities, and possibilities. He couldn't get enough of it. He loved Moody, he loved Chicago, he loved God, he loved preaching, he loved Hilda. He loved life, and it showed. He became a popular student, and his classmates began to understand his deep affection for his girlfriend. They couldn't get him to go on blind dates. The young women who might have chased him were quickly discouraged, and even the good-looking ones didn't turn his head. They might have looked interesting, but he felt God had already given him his intended, and even though he and Hilda hadn't made it official yet, it was settled in his mind.

As if he didn't have enough to do, George was chosen art editor for the *Moody Student,* the campus newspaper. It was during his tenure in that role that he drew a critical cartoon that offended someone. The memory of that haunted him for days, and he took a decided turn against cartoon style artwork and never again employed it.

The month between his junior and senior years was again jammed with speaking engagements, and he found little time to see Hilda. But Hilda decided to apply at Moody, was accepted, and now they would be together during his senior year. He couldn't wait. She was apprehensive, as he had been before his first year, but he just knew everything was going to turn out for the best.

What could go wrong now? Indeed. If only he had known.

7

Storm Clouds

As if George needed anything more than the love of his life added to his already jammed senior year schedule, the September 16, 1944, issue of the campus newspaper, the *Moody Student*, carried his photo and the following article:

> George Sweeting, youthful evangelist and artist, has been appointed associate editor of the Moody Student, according to Russell T. Hitt, director of the Bureau of Promotion.
>
> Last year Sweeting served as [artist], and will continue that work along with his added assignment.
>
> Sweeting is a native of Paterson, N.J., where he graduated from Central High School. He is at present a third year Pastors Course man and has studied in the Chicago Academy of Fine Arts.

Although George recalls serving in that position for at least a brief period, he apparently didn't hold it long enough to have been listed in the mastheads of subsequent issues of the paper. He was busy with his many other projects, of course, but it may have been the physical problems that befell him midterm that forced him to step down.

In that same issue of the school paper, under a column entitled "What Do *You* Think?" freshmen (or first-termers, as they were called) answered the question, "What do you think could be done to make the reception of the first-termers more pleasant?"

Bob Post, a close friend and cutup who had grown up in the same church as George, answered, "Give them air-conditioned rooms and venetian blinds." Bob was a pianist who eventually traveled with George, roomed with him after a short stint at Moody, and became a Southern Baptist evangelist and pastor. George loved him but had to walk carefully as the freshman wore out the carpet between his room and the deans' offices.

Another freshman, Kathryn Leutzinger, didn't realize she was describing George's experience when she answered, "How about someone to meet you at the station and say, 'Here, let me take your trunks for you'—what a help that would be."

Ruth Weinmann answered, "Give them something to do the first couple of days to help them forget their homesickness. If it hadn't been for George Sweeting from my hometown, I don't know what I would have done!"

An example of the nineteen-year-old George Sweeting's early preaching and writing style was exhibited in a later issue of the *Moody Student* in an article he illustrated and wrote. It was called "To Whom Shall We Go?"

In these days of sorrow and heartbreak, we realize that we need someone to go to.

Inborn in every human being is a God-consciousness. Whether a Hottentot in Africa or a soldier in a foxhole, he cries to someone for help. We are not sufficient in ourselves.

Today Europe is battered and broken. Thousands of children are starving; millions of people are homeless, all their possessions vandalized and obliterated.

Men have destroyed one another with a fiendishness which must make the devil envious. Some boys will never return. Some sweethearts will wait in vain. Many babies will never see their fathers. Today is a day of sadness, and heartbreak. *"To whom shall we go?"*

Shall we go to our government? It can give us money. Perhaps it will even award us a medal for gallant service, but it cannot comfort us in our sadness.

Shall we go to our philosophers? No. Their wisdom can bring no comfort.

Shall we go to the world? It has deceived us. Instead of satisfying and giving real peace, it has left us with our hands full of chaff.

Shall we turn to the ways of sin? Shall we go to the swineland, in the far country? Shall we spend our substance in riotous living? Shall we seek to drown our sorrow and heartache? No—all this can never quench the agonizing thirst. All this can never give rest to the weary, heavy-laden soul.

We need someone greater than ourselves. We need someone who will understand. Someone who has already suffered sorrow and death. Someone who loves us and cares for us.

Therefore, *go to Jesus.* He is the One that can meet everyone's need.

To the artist, He is the altogether Lovely One. To the architect, He is the Chief Cornerstone. To the florist, He is the Rose of Sharon. To the electrician, He is the Light of the World. To the newspaperman, He is the Good News. He is all this—and more.

One day the father and mother of a young woman were burned to death. The girl was heartbroken. Two weeks later she received word that her friend had been killed on the battlefield of Europe. Life seemed worthless.

One evening while seeking to forget her sorrows, she wandered into a gospel meeting and took Christ as her Savior. He alone could heal the broken heart. He alone could give truly satisfying peace. He alone could save. If you have been deluded by the empty cisterns of the world, then turn to Jesus only.

> "When purest delights are nipped in the blossom,
> When those we love best are laid low;
> When grief plants in secret her thorn in the bosom,
> Deserted—to whom shall we go?"

To whom shall you go with your soul-haunting sins? They must be forgiven. But who can forgive them? Only Jesus. He is the One who died for you. He is the One who paid the price of sin. I repeat the haunting question. *"To whom shall you go?"*

As you read this article, say, as the prodigal son, "I will arise and go." Do that and heaven will rejoice, and the music will break upon your soul. "Thy sins are forgiven. . . . Thy faith hath saved thee; go in peace."

Neither George nor Hilda remembers who raised the subject first, but sometime late in 1944 they began to wonder about their relationship. Hilda was getting along well as a freshman, and George was as busy as ever. Because of rules and appearances, Hilda could not go out with him on his many speaking, singing, and drawing engagements, but still they found time to see each other between classes, during study time, and in chapel.

Like all the other couples at Moody through the years, they had to watch their public expressions of affection. There was always a dean or a resident adviser or someone to warn them about sitting too close or holding hands too long. And, of course, kissing on campus was strictly forbidden.

For the first few months of the term, George felt he had the best of all worlds. He was busy, active, committed, and running from sunup to sundown. And Hilda was there with him. They had not promised themselves to each other forever, but to them and to everyone acquainted with them, it was a foregone conclusion. They were a couple, they would be a couple, they would get engaged, and they would marry.

But were they right for each other? It seemed so. Their differences were minor, their disagreements few. But what if they were running ahead of the will of God? How could they know? They had never dated anyone but each other. "Do you want to date others?"

"No. Do you?"

"Then?"

"I don't know. Maybe we shouldn't see each other so much or so often."

"You think we should stop dating for a while? See what happens?"

"I don't know. Do you?"

"I don't know."

Neither remembers now who took which side of that discussion, but at some point, both wearied of it. They decided on a moratorium. It would last a month. They would not date at all. If they ran into each other, they would be cordial. If people asked, no, they hadn't actually broken up. They were just stepping back a while.

In Hilda's mind George never missed a beat. She wondered if he could still be thinking about her constantly as he had said in past. It didn't seem so. He appeared busier than ever, running here, going there, doing this, planning that. He used the extra time in more ministry, more projects.

In George's mind Hilda was now suddenly vulnerable, unprotected, available. She would be susceptible to anyone on campus. What if she didn't know any better and was asked out by someone who was not good for her? Worse, what if she was asked by someone who would be perfect for her, better than George Sweeting? He tried not to think about it. He wanted no one else, looked at no one else, thought about no one else. He was busy, sure, but he was living for the day their moratorium ended.

When he saw her in the hallway or in the cafeteria or in chapel, she looked him full in the face and returned his deep gaze. They tried to remember the point of all this. They were to reevaluate their relationship, right? Pray about it. Think about it. See how they did apart from each other. Quit spending so much time together.

Finally, the month was over. They met in the lounge of the women's dorm. He held both her hands in his and asked her what she was thinking. She made him say it first. "I've never been so sure."

"Me either."

The women's dean came by. "Hey, you two! Not so close!"

They dropped hands, smiling, and leaned back from each other. The dean left. They resumed their positions and talked of the future. From that point, there was no turning back, no second thoughts. George did not propose, but they often found themselves talking about the kinds of ministries they wanted and the type of homes they liked. They both wanted a good-sized family, at least three, maybe four children.

They discussed timing. Would they be ready for marriage after George graduated? They thought so. Her studies and his ministries took on a new urgency. He began a theme that has continued throughout his ministry, that the Christian life is a series of new beginnings.

By spring break of 1945, George had spoken all over the Midwest, carting his equipment and luggage by train to Ohio, Indiana, Wisconsin, and Michigan almost every weekend. Over the break he took on an exhausting schedule, which was reported in the April 13 *Moody Student* under the headline "Sweeting Holds Meetings in Michigan Church and Two High Schools."

> A number of young people accepted Christ as their Saviour and many consecrated their lives fully to God as a result of a week of meetings recently conducted by George Sweeting, youthful artist and evangelist.
>
> Sweeting, a member of the [senior] class, held eleven meetings in Berrien Springs Community Church, Berrien Springs, Mich. He led the congregational singing, did chalk drawing, and spoke to a full crowd at every meeting.
>
> At Berrien County High School and Eau Claire High School, George spoke to general assembly groups on "Why I Believe the Bible to Be the Word of God."

George was at the peak of his young life, committed to God with everything going his way. He couldn't have imagined his future looking any brighter. In truth, all he longed for in life was to preach, draw, and marry Hilda Schnell. He was the ultimate optimist, a dreamer whose every vision was coming true.

And then he noticed it. A nagging pain and inflammation in a testicle. Naive and uneducated in such matters, he assumed it might be some sort of a low-grade infection that would fade. But it got worse.

Within thirty days the swelling and pain forced him to visit Dr. Cottrell, one of the two Institute physicians. After only a brief examination, Dr. Cottrell was concerned. "You really should see Dr. Johnson. I'll make an appointment for you at his office at Swedish Covenant Hospital."

"I can't wait until he's on campus?"

"He won't be back here for a couple of days. I wouldn't wait that long."

George shrugged. It was uncomfortable. If one Institute doctor thought the other should examine him and that it couldn't wait two days, who was he to argue? Still optimistic and fighting off any worry that might have been caused by the implications, he allowed Dr. Cottrell to make the appointment.

George decided not to mention anything to Hilda until he knew more. He just hoped his full spring schedule of speaking engagements wouldn't be affected.

Ignorance is bliss.

8

The Ultimate Threat

D r. Cottrell must have known what he was talking about, because by the time George got off the elevated train near Swedish Covenant Hospital two days later, he was nauseated with the pain. Dr. Titus Johnson was a warm, tender, loving man, a Moody alumnus and a former missionary doctor who had founded hospitals in Africa. He had been briefed on George's problem and performed an immediate cursory examination.

He was direct. "It's a tumor. You'll need your parents' permission for us to perform a biopsy and a subsequent operation to remove the growth."

"What's a biopsy?"

"It's a minor operation I'll perform with a local anesthetic. I'll take a small wedge from the tumor, and we'll examine it to determine if it's malignant. Even if it's benign, it has to come out. But I want to be clear with you, George. You could have a very serious problem. If it is malignant, that means it is cancerous and could threaten your life. At the very least, it will destroy your potential to produce children."

"And if it's benign?" asked the eternal optimist.

"Then all you've suffered is your present pain, and there'll be an uncomfortable recovery period after the removal."

"What's your guess, sir?"

"Frankly, son, I don't like it. But let's wait until after the biopsy to worry about it."

Dr. Johnson may have thought he was talking to the wall when he advised a patient not to worry after what he had told him. But if he had known George Sweeting well, he would have known that the young man would leap at the positive possibilities and forget the negatives. Admittedly, they *were* ominous, and the pain and swelling intensified during the brief wait for his parents' permission. Despite all that, George assumed the best.

When he finally checked into Swedish Covenant and was prepped for the biopsy, which required a shave by a registered nurse, he was too ill to even worry about the embarrassment. All he wanted was relief from the pain. But the biopsy, except for a temporary anesthetic, only added to the pain. He headed back to the Institute that afternoon with no appetite, no drive. All Hilda knew was that he was under the weather and needed some rest.

The message came the next afternoon. Dr. Johnson wanted him to check into Swedish Covenant as soon as possible for the surgery. George assumed that meant it was malignant, because it didn't seem there would be such a rush if it weren't. He was right. His next meeting with Dr. Johnson came after he was in a hospital bed with surgery scheduled the following morning. Dr. Johnson was still warm and friendly, but he was not cheerful. "We're going to do the best we can, son. The tumor is large and malignant, and we have no way of knowing yet how widespread is the damage. Our goal is to remove all of it, but then you will have to undergo radiation treatments. We'll talk about that tomorrow."

For some reason, George was still at peace. He had never been the type to get terribly upset about things, and he knew that, at least, he was going to get some relief from the intense pain. He also knew that he loved God as deeply as a young man could and that he was willing to go anywhere and do anything for Him. George was wide open. He said, "Lord, I'll do anything." And he meant it.

The next afternoon, the pain was gone. The anesthetic was in effect, and the tumor was gone. Dr. Johnson was gentle. He put a hand on George's shoulder and asked several questions to determine how he felt and whether he was up to a serious conversation. George assured him he was.

"Son," Dr. Johnson began slowly, "I know you're a Christian and that your eternal house is in order. I need to tell you that you need to think about getting your earthly house in order, too."

"What are you saying?"

"You have loved ones, you have a schedule, you have responsibilities. There are things you'll want to tidy up. You have a girl-friend?" George nodded. "You'll need to be frank with her."

"About not being able to have children, you mean?"

Dr. Johnson ignored the question. "George, I want to start you on a series of radiation treatments where we attempt to kill off any remaining cancerous cells. These treatments are not painful, but they could have serious side effects. You'll lose weight. You'll be sick. You'll be tired. Exhausted. And if the tumor didn't eliminate the possibility of your having children someday, the radiation probably will."

"Is there any option? Do I have to have the treatments?"

"Frankly, George, they are your major chance to see the end of 1945."

"Even with radiation, I might not?"

"My professional opinion?"

"Of course."

"I question whether you'll see the year out."

The following few days of recuperation were ones of serious self-examination. George felt better. It didn't seem to him as if the end were near. He hadn't begun the radiation treatments yet, either. He didn't plead with God to spare him. He accepted the possibility that He might not. But he wanted to make sure that every area of his life was surrendered to Christ, not as a bargaining chip but because he wanted to live out his days—whatever be their number—in full consecration.

To the best of his knowledge, George was right with the Lord. But he didn't want to be blind. He didn't want to miss something just because he hadn't thought of it. He reread Dwight L. Moody's life story and was struck anew by his emphasis on God's love. George prayed, seeking God's face. Was this something He wanted to deal with in George's life?

But love? Was he not a loving person? Was he not aware of the ultimate sacrificial love of the Father in sending His Son to die? And the unconditional love of the Son in being willing to give up His own life? Was there more?

He kept reading and praying. Moody had been committed to God's love. George had to admit that he had a limited concept of love once he got past the love of the Father. He was a preacher of the gospel, a winner of sinners, a standard bearer, a prophet, an evange-list. Love as a specific ministry emphasis, he had to admit, had left him cold. He'd been a scrapper as a child, a Scot, a stoic. Love was emotional, for sissies. It didn't fit in with a man's faith. What kind of a future was there in something as gentle and submissive as love? Wasn't it just an excuse for a gutless kind of faith? Was it in keeping with militant Christianity? He kept reading.

Speaking of love, D. L. Moody said, "I got full of it. It ran out of my fingers. You take up the subject of love in the Bible! You will get so full of it that all you have got to do is open your lips, and a flood of the Love of God flows out."

Slowly George Sweeting experienced the power of God's love. He felt a warm sense of worth and assurance as he prayed, "Lord, this hospital bed is my altar. I want to adjust my life to Your sovereign will. And Lord, if You don't mind, I'd like to be a living sacrifice."

He sensed it was time to write another lifetime goal, only this time he didn't know how long a stretch that might cover. He wrote, "From this moment forward, I commit my life to be a channel of God's love."

There could be no more holding back from Hilda. She had to know everything. George had to take another difficult, painful, scary step. "The doctor feels there's no way I can have children, and I know that a family was one of your dreams. I want to release you from your commitment to our relationship and tell you that I'll understand if this new angle causes you to change your mind."

Hilda never hesitated. "No, we're together. We're going to serve the Lord together wherever He wants us to serve, children or no children."

The radiation treatments were worse than he had expected. He vomited repeatedly, day after day, trying to get a little food to stay down early in the morning and late at night. In thirty days, his weight plummeted more than forty pounds to 128. He thought, *I'm wasting away. I'm dying.* But he didn't talk like that to Hilda when he came back from the treatments white as a sheet and met her in the social room. He decided he would take one day at a time, serve the Lord to the best of his ability, and see if he could make it to age forty. That meant he had a lot to accomplish in a few short years, but for right then he was hoping to outlive Dr. Johnson's prediction.

On Tuesday, May 1, 1945, on his way back to the Institute from yet another radiation treatment that left him exhausted, weak, and nauseated, he sat at an elevated train station reading of the death of Adolf Hitler in the four-cent Chicago *Herald American.* Suddenly, a woman next to him was harassed by a tall stranger. The man had sat on the other side of the woman and put his arms around her.

The woman turned to George, terror in her eyes. "Sir, will you help me?"

George knew he was in no physical condition to help anyone. Hoping the man was just a drunk who didn't know what he was doing, George tried dissuading him with reason. "Hey, the train's coming. Leave her alone!"

The man stood menacingly, and George found himself rising quickly too. The man swung at him, grazing his jaw. *I'm a student at Moody; what am I supposed to do now?* George backed up, and the man swung again, nicking his chin.

Lord, I don't know what to do, but I've got to do something. Calling on the boxing he'd done as a kid, George dropped his newspaper, set himself in the classic position, and returned a right cross to the man's jaw.

The attacker fell, rolled, and dropped off the platform onto the tracks. George had not been bluffing about the train coming. He had felt it, then heard it, and now he saw it.

If the man flopped much farther, the third rail would electrocute him. George looked to see if he would scramble back up onto the platform, but he was out cold. It was one thing to have protected the woman, but to be responsible for a man's death—George leaped down onto the tracks, himself narrowly avoiding the third rail, and wrestled the man to a sitting position. A gash in the back of the man's head bled profusely. The platform was chest high on George, and the man was nearly twice his weight. The sound of the train was deafening as he hooked his forearms under the man's shoulders and pulled him toward the platform.

Suddenly he could go no farther. With the man a deadweight in his arms and the train approaching, he realized the man's shoes were wedged into the tracks. George gave one last pull, yanking the man from his shoes and heaving him onto the platform, then followed close behind.

The train pulled in, the woman boarded, and George sat on the platform, drained. And alone, save for the bleeding, unconscious man at his feet.

As the man began to rouse, the police arrived. George quickly tried to explain. "I was protecting a lady here. She's gone now. I'm a student at the Moody Bible Insti—"

"It's OK, son," one of the officers said. "People on the other side of the platform saw the whole thing and called us. Everything's going to be all right."

They shook the man awake. "Where do you live, buddy?"

"LaSalle Plaza Hotel," he managed.

George froze. That was across the street and three doors up from the Moody Bible Institute. He was convinced the man would see him on the street one day and kill him. The cops told George to go on and that they would contact him if they needed him.

Back at the Institute, Hilda insisted that he inform the dean. Adolph Broman was a man's man. He said, "George, I would have done the same thing you did. If you have to go to court, I'll go with you."

In a few days, George got a letter from the police, informing him that he had been exonerated of any wrongdoing. That was a relief, but there was still the matter of the man living just a few doors down. George had rarely worn a hat before that.

Now he wore one pulled down over his ears and almost over his eyes everywhere he went.

9

Moving On

eorge Sweeting never again saw the tall stranger he had knocked out. Whenever he found himself worrying about the man or his own grave physical condition, he kept himself from becoming overly concerned by claiming Psalm 27:1: "The Lord is my light and my salvation; whom shall I fear? the Lord is the strength of my life; of whom shall I be afraid?" Sometimes he reminded himself, "Lord, You're my light. Lord, You're my salvation. Lord, You're my strength." As his strength slowly returned, so did his courage. Eventually the hat was laid aside.

He had canceled several speaking engagements and had also fallen behind in his studies. He went on an all-out campaign to finish and graduate in August, working hard to catch up with the assistance of several student friends. Most helpful was a young man named Harry Zimmer, who took it upon himself to see that George caught up. Not only did George graduate, but he was also chosen male class speaker for the class exercises. After graduation, he was ordained in his home church.

George was planning to take more classes at the Chicago Art Institute, and Hilda planned to finish the two-year women's course at

Moody. They hoped to be married the next year, shortly after Hilda's graduation. When they were both out of school, George hoped the Lord would lead him into full-time preaching. Then they would start adopting children.

Both having been raised in such close-knit, godly families, however, they felt the need to approach their parents before making any definite plans. It was good that they did, for their marriage would have not been accepted just then, especially by the Schnells, specifically Mr. Schnell. He had always been supportive of the relationship and admired and respected George to the point that he would lend him his car frequently when the couple was home and needed it. But now he had some hard counsel.

"I believe you are too young. I'd prefer that you wait. Then you'll have the Lord's blessing and your parents' blessing."

They were stunned and disappointed, but these were young people who professed to be sold out to God. They knew the scriptural admonition to respect and obey their parents, so after a brief private chat during which they agreed that this could be of the Lord, George asked Mr. Schnell, "How long a wait would you suggest?"

"One year," he said. They swallowed. He continued. "That will give you time to get more schooling, George. Hilda can finish at Moody and then come home for another year."

George and Hilda quietly made their plans. He would study at the Art Institute, as planned. He would also travel and speak as often as possible, trying to employ many of the partners he'd used from Moody when he went out as part of a foursome that called itself variously The Moody Four, The King's Men, and Crusaders for Christ. The team was made up, according to their promotional literature, of "enthusiastic, accomplished" songleader Bill Fusco, "inspiring" keyboard artist Don Van Hoozier, "talented" tenor soloist Merril Booth ("who sings his way into the hearts of his audience"), and the "young, evangelistic, lighting chalk artist" George Sweeting.

Hilda would finish Moody, then return home to work for a year while George went on to Gordon College in Massachusetts. It was not going to be easy, but they knew it would be right. They accepted it as of the Lord, and although they now believe that they could have easily handled the pressures of marriage at that age, their love was only strengthened and deepened by waiting.

George stayed with Bob Post—who did not return to Moody a second year—in a squalid flat just north of the Institute, and those days the neighborhood was dangerous. George remembers sleeping with a hammer tucked under his pillow because their first-floor flat had windows that extended to ground level. The area was rife with prostitution and even white slavery.

Hilda quietly stayed at her studies except when George was free for a brief date. He and Bob, who played the piano and led singing in many of George's meetings, accepted invitations wherever they could. To George, it was simple and straightforward. "Not like today," he says, "where everyone makes it so complicated in trying to find their specific gifts. I never thought about it. I just wanted to serve. I found out what my gifts were when I tried things and people responded to them. If someone told me they received Christ because of one of my sermons or one of my drawings, I thanked God for the gifts He had given me and got on with the task. I was concerned about doing what I was supposed to do. And that was preaching and teaching God's Word and winning people to Christ."

He felt the same way about his life's partner. "Young men come to me today with a list of a dozen things they require in their future wife. I tell 'em, 'You'll never find her. She's not out there. I already married that girl, and there's no more like her out there.' But seriously, I try to get them to back off from their list of requirements a little, to quit looking for someone teachable and start looking in the mirror to see if maybe there isn't something they could learn from a woman, too.

"I tell a young man, if she loves Christ and is a spiritually growing person, determine whether you have spiritual, mental, and physical compatibility and go for it. Spiritual compatibility means that you both love Christ wholeheartedly. Mental compatibility means that you like the same things, and if you don't, that you find out what your intended likes and cultivate a taste, or at least an appreciation, for it. I know the world puts the physical first, but you'll find that it's third as you live your lives, so although it's important, it's not as important as the first two."

For a little privacy with his own intended occasionally, George took Hilda either for a walk on the beaches at Lake Michigan—even when it was too cold for man or beast—or found a secluded spot a few blocks from Moody. George's buddy from Moody days, John Haggai—who would also go on to become a pastor, international evangelist and missionary statesman—often took his fiancée to the same area. When George and Hilda started heading back to the Institute, George would call out, "Let's go, Haggai. Call it a night."

At a luncheon at the Institute a couple of years ago, John Haggai teased Dr. Sweeting about the fact that there should be a plaque down on that street honoring the evenings that George and Hilda stood there smooching. "There would have to be two plaques," George deadpanned.

One of the highlights of George Sweeting's life came near the end of the spring in 1946 when he was contacted by Herrmann Braunlin and invited to speak at the Pavilion that summer. He was dazed by the opportunity. For as long as he could remember he had saved the handsome little brochures that hawked the meetings by showing pictures of each speaker and listing a brief description of the man. The 1945 brochure contained a picture of Billy Graham, along with all the rest of the speakers. Under his photo: "On leave from his thriving [Chicago] church to conduct special nationwide youth rallies. Older folk like him, too."

For his first of several consecutive summers in the Pavilion lineup, George shared the program with such heavyweights as Jack Wyrtzen of New York, Billy McCarrell of Cicero, Illinois (and founder of the Independent Fundamental Bible Churches of America), and A. W. Tozer.

In the flesh, George knew that, as a twenty-one-year-old artist evangelist, he had no business in such a lineup. It would have been next to impossible to enjoy such a break if he had not grown up in that church. Yet his God was the author of the impossible, and he looked forward to that seven-day assignment as he had never looked forward to any before.

Hilda had graduated from Moody and headed home to work in a department store and then switched to the bakery when her father needed her, so she attended the meetings. Her parents did, too, but George's parents did not show up. Hilda wondered if that bothered him, but if it did, he was able to suppress it. He knew they were pleased and proud of him, but they would have thought that by taking the trouble to get out and hear him, they might have been giving him undue honor.

The year wait before the wedding was one of the longest in Hilda's life. George was eager, too, but as usual he was busy. He went on to Gordon College where he began a two-year BA program. As well known in the East as in the Midwest, he was booked solid every weekend with large speaking engagements. He still meets people all over the world who came to Christ at those meetings and have gone on with the Lord, many to lead ministries of their own.

Many people wonder if there's money in itinerant evangelism. Perhaps there is for the unscrupulous, but George never set a fee and always accepted a love offering or a prearranged figure. He recalls that occasionally it was "a big handshake, a thank-you, and a few bucks."

While he was in Berrien Springs, Michigan, in December 1945 for one of his thrice yearly visits there, the crowds swelled every one of the eight nights, and the total love offering was $168. After the meeting he went straight to Peacock's Jewelers in Chicago and put the whole amount on a diamond ring for Hilda. The night he planned to give it to her back in New Jersey, he pulled her father's car into the parking lot of Hawthorne High School. Right in the middle of his routine, a light shined through the window.

"What's going on here?"

"Oh, we're just getting engaged, officer," George said.

"Go home and get engaged," the officer said.

Finally, between George's junior and senior years at Gordon, the big day, June 14, 1947, arrived. After having had their eyes on each other for seven years and waiting a year longer than they had planned, George and Hilda were married at the Hawthorne Gospel Church by Herrmann Braunlin. (Of course, Hilda never complained, but George admits that the ring, even for 1946 money, "was a little dinky." For their thirtieth wedding anniversary in 1977, he had a jeweler friend and member of Moody Church design a beautiful ring for her. "I wanted a good one. I always felt I should have done better for her, though she never would have said anything.")

He and Hilda rented a small, basement apartment in Wollaston, Massachusetts, twenty miles outside Boston, from which they traveled to Maine, Vermont, New Hampshire, Rhode Island, and all through New England for crusades and meetings. She worked in a department store during the week, but they were partners in ministry on the weekends. Hilda played the piano while he drew and sang and preached.

Their posters read: "Presenting George Sweeting in art, word, and song. Evangelist. Artist. Inspiring song service. Drawings. Unique lighting effects. Musical background. A Bible message. Rev. and Mrs. George Sweeting are graduates of the Moody Bible Institute of Chicago. Mr. Sweeting has attended the Art Institute of Chicago and is now studying at Gordon College of Theology in Boston."

That August he was back at the Pavilion with this blurb by his name in the brochure: "God gave us eyes as well as ears. There is double value in his illustrated talks on Gospel truths."

Early in his senior year at Gordon, George was elected class president, unusual for a married student living off campus. He was happy studying, traveling, preaching, and being married. Hilda remembers those days as among the happiest of their lives. Their plan was that after he graduated they would see where God led him in ministry and then think about adopting.

George loved the life of the itinerant evangelist and believed that might be where God was leading him. Indeed, all the doors opened for him, and people responded. He, however, had the nagging feeling that it was difficult for him to understand the local churches and the pastors he served when he dropped in on them for just a few days or a week at a time. He had graduated the pastors course at Moody, and he began considering a grounding in the pastorate before launching a full-time crusade strategy as a life's work and ministry.

Late in December of 1947, Hilda came home from work with the news, "George, I think I'm pregnant." George was overjoyed, but he wondered if she could be right. What were the odds?

The doctor confirmed the news and set the delivery date for August 1948. They knew that if all went well, this would truly be a miracle baby. What they didn't know was where they would be at the time. Would George be traveling, preaching, pastoring, or would he be on scholarship at the Yale School of Missions?

10

Opportunities Abound

In the spring of 1948, George Sweeting had several options. More than a few of the churches he had visited during his hundreds of meetings had asked when he might be available to pastor. He wanted to take a church, but he knew better than to believe he could start as the sole pastor, even if the work was small. Sure, the people might like him, and he had enough common sense to be able to get along with them, but there was so much about the pastorate that he still wanted to learn.

He looked into a few assistant and associate pastor openings, but they weren't offering enough opportunities to preach. He feared he might sound a little demanding, being a newcomer, but what he really wanted—and needed—was an opportunity that would not only afford him the opportunity to preach on a semiregular basis to the same congregation but that would also give him the freedom to continue his evangelistic work.

Early in the spring he was called into the office of the president of Gordon College. With him were two of the top deans. They began by congratulating him on his academic work, his presidency of the class, his new wife, their impending child, and his bright future.

"George, we see you as the kind of a man we would like to head up our world missions department."

George was dazed. "But I, but . . ."

"We know that all the other department heads around here have doctorates. You would need one, too. That's why we're willing to wait. With your enthusiasm, your passion for souls, your preaching and teaching gifts, we're willing to take a chance that you'd be a good administrator, a leader of people, too."

"Well, I appreciate that. I mean, I'm honored. Very flattered, but . . ."

"We know you've been going to school for a lot of years now, but you can get your doctorate in just a few more years. And here's the best part. We'll make it easy for you. You find a place to live close to Yale, and we'll pay your way. Totally. Free ride. Their missions courses are the best of their type in the world. What do you say?"

George shook his head, not wanting to offend. He could appreciate what they were trying to do, and he felt good about the program at Gordon. Whether the Yale missions courses were the best, he couldn't say, but he did know that as impressive as this sounded, it didn't seem to fit in with where God was leading him.

"I'd have to say no, gentlemen. I'm sorry. I just don't think it's me."

"Would you think about it and pray about it?"

"Well, I would, but I don't want to waste your time. You see, I really don't have the inclination toward the purely academic—no offense. I don't think I'm the one for it. I'm not your man. But thank you for your confidence in me."

The Gordon people were disappointed but not unhappy with George's decision. In fact, he sensed that they appreciated his forthrightness and sense of direction. He was correct, of course, that only someone with that inclination would be right for the job. And the one thing he was sure of, as much as he respected education, was that he wanted to preach. "I *had* to preach," he says.

George had always been a firm believer that God saves His very best for those who are willing to wait. Within a few weeks his patience was rewarded. The board of Hawthorne Gospel Church informed him that Pastor Herrmann Braunlin was suffering from bleeding ulcers, and the board was attempting to get him some help so he could pace himself a little better. "We would like to discuss your interest in an associate pastorship here."

George was nearly speechless. He had never been and never would be impulsive on major decisions, even when everything looked too good to be true. As now. He and Hilda prayed about it and felt deep peace. There were still details to be worked out, but after several meetings with the board, he felt from everything he could gather that this was a role that suited him, and vice versa. The board assured him that he would get ample regular preaching opportunities. He informed them that he realized if he accepted, the church would have to be his top priority, but that he was not interested in completely cutting out his own conference and crusade work. They agreed to let him take five outside crusades a year. He also felt the need to inform them that he would not likely be a long-term member of the staff, "Two years at most. I want to take a pastorate, and then I want to travel as an evangelist."

There was one other consideration crucial to George. "I need to know that this is what Pastor Braunlin wants, given my limited commitment. Many fine students and pastoral candidates have come up through his ministry."

"You are his first and only choice. If you will let us put your name before the congregation, we believe they'll ratify our recommendation."

The May 1948 issue of *Fellowship*, Hawthorne Gospel's church newsletter, told the story under the title "Going Forward":

At a special meeting of the congregation on Wednesday, May 5, the members of this church . . . heartily concurred in the choice of George Sweeting for Pastor Braunlin's associate in the work. Mr. Sweeting is a graduate of the Moody Bible Institute, has taken special studies at the Art Institute of Chicago, and will graduate from Gordon College this June. He has done extensive work as a chalk artist evangelist. He will come to Hawthorne early in July. He will conduct half the daily Inspiration Time broadcasts, preach at most of the Sunday evening evangelistic meetings, teach in the Hawthorne Evening Bible School, and take some of the outside meetings at which our pastors have opportunity to meet radio friends.

During his last month at Gordon, George sent a message to the congregation, which appeared in the church newsletter in June 1948:

"For we preach not ourselves but Christ Jesus the Lord; and ourselves your servants for Jesus' sake" (2 Corinthians 4:5).

Some time ago my wife and I took this as our life's verse. The word "servants" in the original means "to bind." Paul speaks here of one who is bound to another. Because of past experiences and memories, we feel bound in a peculiar way to the people and pastor of the Hawthorne Gospel Church. With the help of God we are looking forward to great days ahead. We are grateful indeed to be bondslaves of Christ forever.

Upon graduation from Gordon, George and Hilda returned to Hawthorne and George immediately immersed himself in the work. He handled all the Sunday evening preaching and half of the radio broadcasts; taught Old Testament, New Testament, and public speaking Mondays in the Hawthorne Evening Bible School; and taught a hundred men in Sunday school. That was all on top of the youth work and a complete restructuring of the Sunday school program—times, teachers, classrooms, and all.

On Sunday morning, August 8, while Vance Havner was preaching the morning service, George David Sweeting was born. George and Hilda called him their miracle baby. A few years later, when they'd had four sons, George ran into Dr. Titus Johnson in Chicago. The old physician threw his arms around George. "There's no medical explanation for it, you know. Those are truly miracle children."

Besides also preaching later that month at the Pavilion (this time his brochure blurb read: "His fine messages, skillfully illustrated in color, won our Pavilion audiences last summer"), he picked up the visiting speakers and hosted them during their individual weeks of ministry. It was a privilege to meet Vance Havner, Merv Rosell, Bob Pierce, John Walvoord, Carl Armerding, A. W. Tozer, and the rest. He squeezed from them all the advice he could, and then for weeks afterward he found himself preaching like each one.

The greatest benefit George felt he received during his eighteen-month stay at Hawthorne was the tutelage of Herrmann Braunlin. Braunlin had not been trained to be a pastor. He had taken on the fledgling work at the urging of Pastor Drew at Madison Avenue Baptist, and for the first ten years he gave the church a running start, supporting himself fully by working as a bookkeeper in New York City.

George found him relaxed, methodical, not flashy. He was committed to seeing his congregation learn the Word, and he was never hesitant to bring in the big names to preach to them. His twelve-hour days set the pace for the entire staff. He was self-effacing, insisting on being voted upon every year. He was steady and never lost his cool. Throughout his ministering life, George always asked himself, after taking a problem to God in prayer, "What would Herrmann Braunlin do?"

The *Fellowship* newsletter from that period shows that George did a lot of preaching in the area, besides being involved with virtually every area of the church life. At the end of 1948 he wrote in the newsletter a message called "The Year 1949":

> We are standing on the brink of a new year. Not one of us knows what the future holds. But here is the joyous, gladdening message—we know the One who holds the future.
>
> The oriental shepherd was always ahead of his sheep. He led them so that any attack on them had to deal with him first. So our Lord GOES BEFORE.

> "Dangers are nigh! and fears my mind are shaking;
> Heart seems to dread what life may hold in store;
> But I am His—He knows the way I'm taking;

More blessed still—He goes before."
The past year has been one of tremendous change. World events
have literally tumbled over each other. A cynic has remarked that nothing is permanent except change.

"Change and decay in all around I see;
Oh, Thou Who changest not, abide with me!"

We should be thankful for a changeless Christ in a changing
world. How shall we face the new year?
Let us face the NEW YEAR with the OLD BOOK; face the
NEW NEEDS with the OLD PROMISES; and face the NEW PROB-
LEMS with the OLD GOSPEL.

Truly, George and Hilda did not know what was in store for
them or their friends in 1949. The February *Fellowship* letter
announced that George's old friend Bob Post and his wife, Helen,
were moving to Lancaster, South Carolina, where Bob became musical director of the Second Baptist Church, of which John Haggai was
pastor.

Later in the year, George sought a new opinion on his health. On
September 16, he received a letter from a Willet F. Whitmore Jr.,
M.D., of New York City, which said, in part: "The fact that you have
remained free of any symptoms . . . is in itself pretty good evidence
that the tumor has been eradicated." From that point on, George
never looked back.

In the autumn, a call was extended to George to become pastor of
the two-hundred-member Grace Church in Passaic, New Jersey.
From the first, the offer excited him. It had come earlier than he had
planned to leave. They wanted him by the first of the year. The work
was going so well at Hawthorne that he knew some people would not
understand. He went through deep pain trying to decide. One of the
first things he did was to assess what he had learned from Pastor
Braunlin and develop his own philosophy of pastoring. First, he says,
a pastor should model the Christian life to his people. They learn best

by example. Values are easier to exemplify than to teach. The greatest contribution a pastor can make to his people is the example of a godly life. Integrity is the name of the game.

Second, George wanted to be a channel of God's love to a congregation. He believed that a proclamation and an illustration of God's love through the pastor would solve 95 percent of the problems churches face. Loving God and loving one another is key to a smooth-functioning church.

Third, he believed that nothing could take the place of thorough preparation to teach or preach. His advice to young pastors: be overprepared. If a pastor is prepared and tuned in to what's happening in the world, people will beat a path to his door. So, he says, master the Bible and know the times in which we live.

Fourth, surround yourself with a highly qualified, exciting, spirit-filled team that serves the people and serves the Lord, expecting God to do great things. An attractive music program is a plus, as is a comprehensive approach to Christian education, but George feels these are subservient to the four major points.

It had been a thrill for George to have worked in his home church, even knowing that the time would be short. Two women in the church, when they heard he was trying to make the big decision, informed him in writing and in person that he was clearly out of the will of God. He informed them that Paul had served at Corinth only eighteen months and went back to agonizing prayer about the decision.

He penned his letter of acceptance, then he and Hilda drove to Passaic to drop it in the slot in the front door of Grace Church. When they arrived, however, chest pains and what he calls a "lack of courage or guts or strength to do it" gripped him, and he couldn't get out of the car.

"Do you feel you're to go?" Hilda asked gently.

"Yes."

"Shall we pray?"

"Please."

When she finished praying, she studied him. "George, do you want me to put the letter in the slot?"

11

One More Step

ilda Sweeting's trotting up the steps to the front door of Grace Church in Passaic, New Jersey, and dropping her husband's letter through the mail slot was not a foreshadowing of her role in the marriage. Then, as now, George took the lead, consistent with their view of Scripture on the spiritual headship of the husband. When they have a decision to make, especially on an important issue, they wait until both are agreed and then they go ahead.

The move to Passaic was one such issue. "I knew he felt strongly," Mrs. Sweeting says, "and I did, too. For some reason he just had a very difficult time putting that letter in. All I wanted to know was whether he really felt he was to go. He was in turmoil partly because of the actions of those two friends at Hawthorne who didn't want him to leave, and I was glad to help him through it."

Herrmann Braunlin couldn't have been more supportive, as evidenced in the December 1949 *Fellowship* newsletter: "Pastor Sweeting has announced to the church that he feels led of God to accept a call to become pastor of Grace Church in Passaic, NJ. He will continue his work in Hawthorne until the end of the year."

Commenting on the announcement, Pastor Braunlin said, "The

Lord was good in permitting us to have Pastor Sweeting with us. It was understood when he came that his ministry with us was temporary. His contribution to the work in Hawthorne has been very valuable. May the blessing of God be on him in his new ministry in Passaic. And may He bless Hilda and George [David], too."

In the same issue, George penned a farewell message:

> The Hawthorne Gospel Church has played a tremendous role in the life of our family. So much so that it has become part of us.
>
> As young people, Mrs. Sweeting and I attended this church. Both of us dedicated our lives here to serve the Lord. It was here that we followed the Lord in baptism and shortly after became members of the fellowship. Both of us were graduated from the Moody Bible Institute. Between my junior and senior years [at Gordon] we were married in— that's right, Hawthorne!
>
> Eighteen months ago we returned home to take up our labor among you. How we thank God for your cooperation in spreading the Gospel from the first even until now! For your kindnesses and love we shall always be grateful. The Lord has been so good that we could not begin to count our blessings.
>
> And now it is time on God's clock for us to move on to new places. Our consolation is this, "He holds the key to all unknowns and we are glad. If other hands should hold the key, we would be sad."
>
> Only a strong sense of conviction that we are doing the right thing orders us to take this step.
>
> With Paul we would say: "I thank my God upon every remembrance of you, always in every prayer of mine for you all making request with joy, for your fellowship in the gospel from the first day until now; being confident of this very thing, that he which hath begun a good work in you will perform it until the day of Jesus Christ" (Philippians 1:3-6).
>
> Gratefully, and prayerfully,
> Pastor George Sweeting

One of the major reasons the Passaic church was attractive to George Sweeting was its location. He had long believed that the city was a prime element in God's strategy to reach the masses. He studied D. L. Moody's approach to cities and became convinced that if the gospel can reach the cities, it will reach the greatest number of people in the shortest time.

The two years the Sweetings spent in Passaic solidified George's unflagging commitment to the inner city. Thirty-five years later it had become synonymous with his approach to evangelism. He is missions-minded and thankful for the thousands of Moody alumni who serve in remote parts of the earth—another stratagem he knows is indispensable, particularly for Scripture translation—but his heart and mind and tendency is toward the masses in the cities of the world. While president at Moody he sharpened the Institute's city focus and kept that emphasis before the trustees, the faculty, the staff, the students, and the constituency.

Occasional offers came from wealthy donors to move the Institute to beautiful country settings, but George's view was that the Moody Bible Institute was not in the city by accident. It was not there simply because that happened to be where Moody founded the place. "We're not stuck here," Dr. Sweeting would say. "We're here because God called us here, because we feel He has a special concern for the city, a special concern for the individual, yes, and also for the masses."

Little documentary material is available from George Sweeting's first senior pastorate, but clearly it was a two-year stint of meteoric accomplishment. Many of those parishioners have remained friends of the Sweetings. Those who attended from 1950 through early 1952 agree that it was akin to a twenty-four-month evangelistic crusade. Hundreds were converted, were baptized, and became members, and scores of others grew in their dedication to Christ. In two years the church doubled in size.

It was not without roadblocks, however. One member recalls that the young preacher was single-mindedly making changes, introducing new programs and procedures, and generally waking up a resting congregation. There were those for whom the changes were upsetting, coming too fast. At a women's prayer meeting one morning, some woman began to pray that the Lord would "help this pastor who's bringing in all these modern, newfangled ideas."

George happened to pass the door and heard the tirade. "Ladies!" they heard suddenly. A dozen heads raised, and two dozen eyes popped open. "Up! Go home! This prayer meeting is not a place for gossip! Go home!" They went in tears, but the controversy stopped there. None were lost to other churches, and the congregation grew to support George's efforts.

Being willing to confront is a prerequisite to effective leadership, and although George developed a reputation as a master at it, he admits he has disliked it all his life. He is suspicious of those to whom it comes easy to call on the carpet, discipline, or fire someone. He admires those who can do it, but he doesn't employ those who enjoy it. He considers them dangerous, with problems of their own.

Curiously, those subordinates who have been reprimanded by Dr. Sweeting over the years have not been aware of his distaste of the necessity of such encounters. It's not that they believe he enjoys it, but they agree that he does it with such tact and thoroughness that it belies the sleeplessness he has suffered in advance.

A former Moody Bible Institute employee tells the story of being summoned to Dr. Sweeting's office without a clue as to the reason. He could tell immediately from Sweeting's kind but formal air that something was amiss. When the president began a rundown of the employee's offense, using carefully prepared, handwritten notes on a yellow legal pad, the accused's memory was refreshed. He says his reason, his excuse, his explanation begged to be offered. "But, sir, yes, I . . ."

At that point Dr. Sweeting looked up from his notes with apparent surprise at the interruption. "Excuse me," he said, gently using the perpetrator's first name, "but when I am finished you'll have an opportunity to speak."

"Not an opportunity to explain why it happened," the victim recalls with a wry smile. "An opportunity to accept the responsibility

George Sweeting was born in the home at left on October 1, 1924. To the right is the Haledon Grammer School the Sweeting siblings attended.

Margret Hilda Schnell Sweeting's childhood home. Her parents ran the attached bakery.

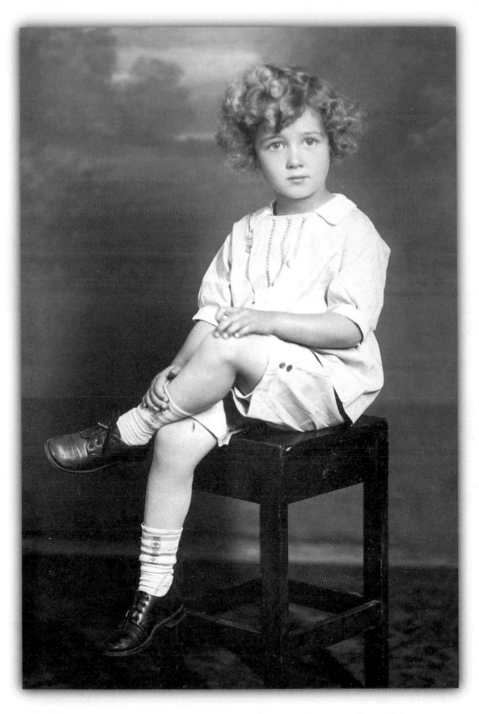

In the European tradition, Mr. and Mrs. William Sweeting let young George's hair grow untill he was approximately four years old.

Mr. and Mrs. William Sweeting (back) with (L to R): Anne, George (age 9 in 1934), Norman, and William.

George, at 17, bears a striking resemblence to his own son Don, except for the hair style and color.

Back row (L to R): Norman, William, Anne, and George.
Front row: Martha, Mrs. Mary Sweeting, Mr. William Sweeting, and Mary.

Preaching to the youth of Moody Church while a student at the Institute, 1943.

George Sweeting as an
artist-evangelist–1948

Word of Life
Conference 1948
(L to R) Jack Wyrtzen,
Larry McGuill, Gil Dodc
Front: George Sweeting
V. Raymond Edman,
Carlton Booth

Pinebrook Conference 1954
(L to R) Paul Scheetz, Percy
Crawford, Hilda Schmiezer,
Anthony Zeoli, Alan Forbes,
George Sweeting, Harold
DeCow

George and Hilda at a school banquet in 1945.

The newlyweds, June 14, 1947, with Mr. and Mrs. Osward Schnell (left) and Mr. and Mrs. Sweeting.

Fun in a photo booth.
Still very much in love, 1955.

Clockwise from upper left: Hilda, James Douglas, Donald William, Robert Bruce, George David, and Dr. Sweeting.

Dr. Sweeting was willing to pose for this gag, but not to follow through with the eating.

With Dr. Billy Graham and George Beverly Shea at the institute in 1979.

The Sweeting brothers and their wives (L to R): Bill and Carol, Amelia and Norm, Hilda and George.

1983 – Preaching in Korea with Billy Kim.

Dr. Sweeting honors Dr. Herrmann G. Braunlin as Pastor of the Year for 1980. Dr. Braunlin pastored Dr. and Mrs. Sweeing's home church in New Jersey for more than 62 years. In the background is soloist Burt Kettinger.

The Rev. Billy Kim translated Dr. Sweeting's messages each evening at the evangelistic crusade in Inchon, 1983.

Bob, Don, Jim, and, George gather at their father's 60th birthday surprise party in Chicago, 1984.

With Dr. Francis Schaeffer, shortly before Schaeffer's death.

Chicago Mayor Harold Washington was a guest at the Moody
Bible Institute in 1984. At right is Marvin Beckman, MBI vice
president and general counsel.

Sharing with Yitsak Rabin, Prime Minister of Israel.

Dr. Sweeting began the Moody Pastor's Conference in 1972. This picture was taken in 1982.

On the balcony outside his ninth floor office, Dr. Sweeting chats with his successor, Dr. Joseph M. Stowell.

Chuck Colson and
Dr. Sweeting

Dr. Sweeting with Dr. Bill Bright

George Sweeting with Luis Palan

1984 – Dr. Sweeting with President and Nancy Reagan.

From L to R Louis Solheim, Dr. Sweeting, Louise Solheim and Karsten Solheim of the Ping Golf family.

Ruth and Billy Graham, Hilda and George Sweeting at the Graham home in 1994.

The Sweeting family at the dedication of the Sweeting Center for World Evangelism.

Dr. Sweeting throwing out the first pitch at Wrigley Field in 1998.

George Sweeting crusading for souls.

Jerry Jenkins, special friend and M.C. for the Sweeting's 50th wedding anniversary.

Celebrating 50 Years of marriage – June 14, 1997

and keep my job. I felt worse about having interrupted the master-piece of a dressing-down than I did about what had caused it. When he looked at me with those blue eyes under that pure white hair and excused himself for interrupting my interruption, I wanted to crawl under the chair. If I'd had a shovel, I'd have gone from the ninth floor to the basement in a minute. And when he did finish, explaining why what I had done was unacceptable and telling me that he knew I was a better manager than I had showed, all I could do was use my 'oppor-tunity to speak' not to try to explain myself but simply to assure him why it would never happen again."

Others say that George was capable of being chilly for long peri-ods, either before he had prepared his litany of offenses or before he had talked himself into facing the ordeal. "By the time he finally calls you in," one says, "you're practically begging him to do it. The chewing out is much less painful than the cold shoulder, the constant reminder that you have disappointed."

In spite of the ringing success of the Grace Church pastorate, George still felt called to itinerant evangelism. Strangely, for all the ministering he was doing in that church, the calling, the teaching, the training, the counseling, and the administration, preaching twice on Sunday and at least once in the middle of the week simply wasn't enough. If there was one thing that had been branded on his heart at the David Otis Fuller meeting in 1940, it was that he had been called to preach, to proclaim the gospel. He wanted to do that every chance he got. He wanted to preach the Word on as close to a daily basis as he could.

The pastorate, for all its challenges and complexities, has to be—from a pragmatic standpoint—easier than traveling to a different church every week, being gone from your family, living out of a suit-case. In traveling there is the advantage that you can leave your best and first impression and know you'll be moving on in eight or fifteen or thirty days, but the reward of not having to stay in one place and deal with difficult personalities is small compensation for the hard-ships of life on the road.

Yet it fit in with George's calling. His goal since studying at

Moody had been to preach, and he had at every opportunity. Every other task he had was secondary to the preaching of the gospel. He did it on weekends while a student, whenever he could as an associate pastor, and as often as he could get away while a pastor. The call became more urgent. He had to preach and preach and preach, and the prospect of doing it full-time, as his own boss, with his own staff, setting his own schedule, whetted his appetite. With every passing week, though the work was exhilarating at Grace, he felt more and more drawn to full-time evangelism.

While in Passaic, the Sweetings had their second son, James Douglas. They felt doubly blessed, of course, with yet a second miracle baby. It did give George and Hilda pause, however, about George's plan to be gone so much of the time. Her parents insisted that if they followed through with the intention, they move in with the Schnells, who now lived in Ridgewood. That would cut expenses and give Hilda and the babies support company during the week.

That might appear as strange to the modern mind as waiting a year to get married just because the parents requested it, but again, George and Hilda were not worried about conventional wisdom. They wanted to follow God, and this seemed to be of Him. The Schnells loved George deeply and wanted him to succeed. There was no pre-set limit to the arrangement. No one knew how long George would be on the road or when the Sweetings might have another child. (When Donald William was born in 1955, they would move to their own home in Wyckoff, New Jersey.) For then, it was simply the best plan, and it was to work better than any outsider would have predicted.

The local paper carried the announcement under the headline "Grace Church Pastor Gives Up Pulpit; Rev. George Sweeting Leaving to Become a Traveling Evangelist":

> The clergyman will preach his farewell sermon at the evening service, January 27. An informal farewell gathering for church members and friends will be held January 24.
>
> After February 1, the Rev. Mr. Sweeting will begin an evangelistic tour of the East and Midwest. His tentative schedule for this year

includes appearances before Baptist church groups in Chicago, Boston, and Bluefield, W. Va., and before Baptist and independent church audiences in Greenville, S.C.

Several television appearances also are planned for the young pastor, who adds visual interest to his sermons by on-the-spot drawings of topics from his text.

During the Rev. Mr. Sweeting's travels, his wife and their sons will live with her parents, Mr. and Mrs. Oswald Schnell, 115 South Maple Avenue, Ridgewood, former Fairlawn residents.

Under the Rev. Mr. Sweeting's ministry, the Grace Church enlarged its auditorium and purchased and remodeled a house adjacent to the church building to provide room for church functions. Sunday school attendance grew from 190 to an average of 360 students at weekly classes, and two new buses were purchased to provide transportation for pupils. In the last year, the church donated $17,000 to missionary purposes.

Meanwhile, its pastor received requests for appearances at city-wide meetings and church revival services in more than 100 cities. This fall he has been invited to minister in Europe under Youth for Christ of Great Britain. . . .

He was ordained at Hawthorne Gospel Church in 1945 and served as associate pastor there two years. He is the son of Mr. and Mrs. William Sweeting, of Haledon, who have two other sons in the ministry. William, the eldest, was formerly pastor of Brookfield Baptist Church, Chicago, and is professor of theology at Providence Bible Institute, Providence, R.I. Norman, the youngest son, attends Faith Theological Seminary, Wilmington, Del.

Mrs. Sweeting, who serves as organ or piano accompanist for her husband's illustrated sermons, is the former Hilda Schnell. The couple have two sons, George David, three, and James Douglas, 11-months old.

George couldn't wait to get started.

12

Brother Greeney and His Blackboard

*H*ilda Sweeting disliked being alone, so moving in with her parents was a godsend. She still missed her husband terribly, of course. In later years people mistakenly assumed that it was easier for her when George was away because she had got used to it during the near decade he traveled as an evangelist. Not so, she says. "I think that's one thing you never get used to."

She knew he was going to be gone a good deal, but she didn't know how long he would stay in the ministry as a traveling evangelist. Fortunately, her father was so concerned about her welfare—and George's—that he always urged her to let him go with her whenever she had to pick George up at the airport or train station. "He didn't want me going alone," she says. "And it didn't make any difference what time of the day or night, my father was always willing to go along."

George organized a group called Sweeting Crusade, Inc., and began church-centered campaigns in which one significant church would sponsor and seek cooperation from others. In the early days it was not uncommon to start on a Sunday night and go fifteen nights through two more Sundays. Some crusades even went for five Sundays with four weeks of preaching. It was exhausting, but it was also invigorating for George. It was what he felt called to do.

There were also those crusades with no major church but several cooperating together. "They could be great," George says, "or they could be a fiasco. Too often everybody's business is nobody's business. You're better to have one good church, gung ho behind you, knowing that it rises or falls with them, than fifty churches committed in name only."

Almost immediately he was booked three years solid, mostly, he feels, because of the double attraction of artistry and preaching. He started by presenting a biblically related chalk rendering on a six-foot board in about twelve minutes, then finished by preaching on that subject while the lights accented and highlighted the artistic illustration. He designed his own easels, which were copied by others in the same field. His books *How to Be a Chalk Artist* and *Ideas for the Chalk Artist* went to press more than twenty times and were used around the world.

George, however, always felt chagrined by the title "Chalk Talk Artist." He clearly had a biblical, spiritual gift of evangelism and was called to that, and he also considered himself an artist. Chalk artists are sometimes considered the stepchildren of "legitimate" artists, but he lived with it because it attracted people to the gospel. That didn't make it any easier the night that a local elder was called upon to pray at the beginning of the meeting and included a request that the Lord "bless Brother Greeney and his blackboard."

George purchased a large tent that was transported from city to city by tractor-trailer with "Christ Is the Answer" painted on the sides. Harold DeCou, organist at Word of Life in New York, traveled with him as keyboard artist, and Irv Chambers often led the singing. If it was a smaller meeting, sometimes George handled both the singing and preaching.

Upon arrival at a church, George first met with the pastor and the board and outlined his approach. He was not there to raise or make money, to be able to brag about huge numbers, or to coerce people into making emotional or short-lived decisions. He just wanted to be a channel of God's love, proclaiming the saving grace of Christ, and inviting people to allow the Holy Spirit to have sway in their lives.

He always told the churches he wanted a minimum of fifty counselors—married couples, singles, even teenagers. He trained them on how to lead a person to Christ, how to answer people's objections, how to avoid making their decision for them, and how to pray with them.

George asked for a hundred volunteers to help erect the tent, and he appointed five foremen. One crew worked on the gully around the tent, another put up the poles, another the canvas and ropes, another worked on the platform, and another on the PA and lighting system. "I gained tremendous experience in how to work with men," he says. "The ones who volunteered for this kind of work were often the blue-collar workers in the churches, and they appreciated being talked to like men. I think they also appreciated the fact that I was right in there with them, lifting, digging, hammering, pulling, hoisting. It took a while to put that tent up, but the same guys, knowing what they were doing, could get it down and loaded on the truck in a few hours, and it would be on its way to the next crusade."

In all the years George used the big tent, he never had one blown down during the actual service, but occasionally one was blown to smithereens by a thunderstorm when a service was over. Once during a meeting in Hammond, Indiana, the winds were so high that George asked that an usher be assigned to hang onto each pole and to put his weight into holding it down. As the canvas started flapping and billowing, one side pole would pull up six feet off the ground and hurtle back to earth, and then the other side pole would do the same. Meanwhile, the ushers wrapped their arms around the poles and rode them up and down as if on a carousel. George preached fast that night.

Anywhere from a thousand to four thousand could be housed in the big tent by adding sections. George also carried the row ends and lumber for benches and seat backs, and the bigger the crowd, the closer together he placed the rows. The portable platform, organ, and PA system fit right on the truck, along with the Sweeting Crusade hymnbooks. The Canvas Cathedral was a novelty all its own in those days and drew many people out of curiosity alone.

On a pole near the platform, George once attached a thermostat that was not, of course, hooked up to anything. There was no source of warmth in the tent except body heat. At the beginning of a meeting on a chilly night, he asked for a show of hands of those who were cold. Everyone responded. "In that case, I'm going to set the thermostat to seventy-five." A few minutes later, after a song or two, he asked how many were comfortable. At least half were. Ten minutes later a request came from the back to turn down the heat a little!

That bit of psychological legerdemain was a harmless bit of showmanship that most understood, but real trickery or deception never became part of George's approach. Some evangelists were not above saying they saw raised hands during an invitation when, in truth, none had been raised yet. They justified that by saying that no one wants to be first, so if they pretended that others had responded, it might draw out a reticent repenter. George never resorted to that, and in fact would not even drag out an invitation hymn any farther than he had announced. If he said they would sing three verses, that's all they sang.

He changed the invitation hymn each night, and he would say, "While we stand to sing, if the Lord has spoken to you, I would urge you to go to the counseling room. We have fifty counselors here, and they will lead the way." He adds, "That made it easier for them to respond. I wouldn't plead with them. I hardly said anything between verses."

His aim in preaching, he says, has always been to "fill them and thrill them. I never wanted to just impart knowledge. Teaching is important, and we ought to present solid material. But I wanted to present the truth to the listener so that he was so excited he couldn't wait to get out of that place and share it with someone else."

George admits that he and Harold DeCou—who went on to become a noted composer and arranger—had a lot of old-fashioned fun driving all over the country, working with pastors and churches, setting up and taking down the tent, and just enjoying each other's

Christian fellowship. During one meeting, Harold fell ill at the organ with food poisoning. Within a few minutes, George also collapsed and was carried out. By the end of the service, the song leader too was rushed to the hospital by ambulance. All had ptomaine poisoning.

George had fun teasing Harold, who was single, from the platform. After introducing him, George occasionally told audiences, "You know, Harold loves cherry pie, and if he could find a girl who could bake a good one, I think he'd marry her." The next night, the platform would be lined with cherry pies. When Harold got a chance to say anything, he'd add, "George is married, but he sure loves apple pie." The next night, all the older women who felt sorry for the lonely, young husband brought apple pies.

Once, George and Harold left a week of meetings with a half dozen pies in the backseat of the car. On that occasion there was no one to give them to and not enough time to eat them all before they spoiled, so when they got out into a deserted country area, they took turns seeing who could throw them the farthest. They threw each like a discus, making those pies forerunners to the Frisbee. "Then we felt so guilty about all those friends who were so kind," George admits, "we never asked for pies again."

(Harold eventually married a girl from Brookfield, Illinois, who baked him a cherry pie. They've been together more than forty years.)

In the spring of 1952, George teamed up with an old friend and accomplice, the man who preceded him as associate pastor at Hawthorne Gospel, to hold a crusade in his old stomping grounds. The April–May Hawthorne Gospel Church *Fellowship* newsletter read:

> Many North Jersey churches are uniting in support of the evangelistic campaign now in progress in the "Big Tent" on Broadway (one mile west of Main Street in Paterson). Larry McGuill and George Sweeting are the two evangelists, sharing the preaching and contributing their talents of music and art. Both evangelists are well known in

this area. The meetings began with a Sunday afternoon meeting at 3 o'clock on May 11, and will continue every night until Monday, June 1.

Keen interest has been shown. A volunteer ushers group has been organized; musicians and singers from the area will assist in the meetings; and many organizations are cooperating.

By this time George had written two books: *The Tongue—Angel or Demon* and *You Can Be a Chalk Artist*. He turned twenty-eight that October and had already spoken in more than a thousand high school and college programs and appeared on television programs across the nation. He spoke daily in army and air bases, civic clubs, and even factories. Wherever he would be heard, he preached. In 1953 his team would conduct 164 high school and college programs.

George joined the Woodland Park Baptist Church, Chattanooga, where John Haggai pastored, to give him entree into Southern Baptist churches and rallies. His promotional material advertised "Persuasive preaching. Beautiful paintings made before your eyes. Music with a message. Clear cut invitations. No advance financing. Effective follow up. Tent equipment owned. Write for open dates. United association-wide, interdenominational, and local church campaigns."

By the next year George was convinced he would be an evangelist all his life. When he considered the pastorate again, he was convinced he was too sensitive for the role. He saw so many pastors tied in knots trying to please everyone, and he didn't feel he had the temperament for it. He wrote several more books during the fifties, including *The Secret of a Happy Home, Life Minus Love Equals Nothing, Mixed Marriage, Why I Believe the Bible to Be the Word of God*, and a sequel to *You Can Be a Chalk Artist* called *Ideas for the Chalk Artist*. When the family book came up for reprint, he asked the publisher to shelve it. "When I wrote it I thought I knew all the answers. By then I knew a happy family was due primarily to the grace of God."

13

International Impact

*B*eginning in 1953, George traveled overseas about every third year. He felt he owed a debt to Scotland and Germany for his and his wife's heritages, and he ministered in orbital countries as well. In Berlin he preached in forty-five refugee camps where people escaped communist areas and fled to the free zone. He and Larry McGuill also preached in several U.S. armed forces bases in Germany. In Scotland, George looked up his paternal grandparents, then in their eighties. He and his brothers and sisters had written to them weekly as children but never expected to see them. It was the early spring of 1953, and Scotland was cold. Their little apartment had a fireplace in every room, but only one was burning. They huddled near it, and George's grandmother brought out tea and scones (tea cakes). Although the Scots generally hide their emotions, it was clear that Grandpa and Grandma Sweeting were thrilled to see their grandson for the first time.

As he began to reminisce about how much he had heard about them, how much his father had respected and admired and loved them, and how grateful George was to them for the way they had influenced and poured their lives into his father, they began to weep.

"He truly loves you," George told them. "You mean so very much to him."

George sensed that they were so warm and tender at that moment that he said he was most grateful that his father had come to Christ and had helped all his children become Christians at young ages. "One of the prayers of his life was that you too might see you need a Savior." George included the entire plan of salvation in his conversation and felt a definite leading of the Lord. "Would you like to commit your lives to Jesus Christ?"

His grandparents said yes in unison, and next to that fireplace in their home in Scotland they prayed. When George returned to the States and told his father, it was the first time George had ever seen him moved with emotion. His father had, of course, tried to witness to his own parents, but for one reason or another there was little response. The time had not been right. Two years later George's father died at age sixty-two. His grandfather died the same year at ninety.

Over the years George has been able to tell that story as an illustration of how love is supportive. He recommends to students that they try to think of several people who have had a significant influence in their lives, then write to them and tell them. Thank them. See what witnessing opportunities might come of it. While a student at Moody, George wrote to thank a man who gave him a job and bought him his first history book. He told the man how he had developed a lifelong interest and fascination with history partly because of that. The man was so impressed that he gladly welcomed George into his home when he was back for a visit. George had the privilege of leading that man to Christ, too.

In May 1955, George and his team had a campaign in Kentucky, which was covered in the *Russellville News-Democrat* under the headline "More than 2000 Attend 'Crusade' in Warehouse":

General widespread interest in the Sweeting Crusade continues to highlight this meeting, sponsored by 55 churches of three Baptist associations in Logan, Simpson, and Todd Counties. More than 2,000 persons attended the opening service Sunday night and over 1,500 Monday night, despite a last minute change in location, due to unfavorable weather conditions. Because of muddy soil at the fairgrounds, it was impossible to use the big tent, and the revival is being held at the New Burley Tobacco Warehouse near the intersection of Bowling Green and Franklin Roads.

Volunteers who had worked long hours effecting the change, arranging for parking and erecting the organ and benches, declared they were more than repaid by the enthusiastic reception given the opening messages of the Rev. Mr. Sweeting and his assistants, Harold DeCou and Irv Chambers.

Bus service, which is being given on all sections having paved roads, is bringing in near capacity loads. . . .

The Rev. Mr. Sweeting has stated that his messages are for all, and in accordance with his belief and practice, will be acceptable to all, regardless of church background.

Rededication on the part of church members has been an outstanding theme of the messages, with an urgent plea for a general spiritual awakening in this section.

There were dangers, temptations, and pitfalls associated with itinerant evangelism, however. George began suffering various maladies from hemorrhoids to loss of hair and from digestive complications to chest pains. The doctors always ascribed them to tension or stress, explaining that his heart was fine but that his hard-driving activities contributed to the symptoms.

In those days it was not unusual for him to drive from New York to Florida for an eight-day crusade, then drive to Colorado for another one. "You don't realize it at the time," he says, "but you build up tension on the way to these things. There was a lot to think about, a lot to keep track of. We always wanted integrity and excellence to be our hallmarks, and that required a great deal of detail work."

One of his great disappointments was running into other evangelists whose motives were other than kingdom-related. George remembers having gone out for a snack with one evangelist after a crusade. "The Lord blessed tonight," George said.

"I don't want to talk shop," the other said.

"Shop?"

"Yeah, shop! Let's not. Let's talk about girls."

"Let's not," George said. "The only 'girl' I ever wanted is in New Jersey waiting for me." That evangelist eventually accepted an offer to become a nightclub performer and was dead of alcoholism by age forty-five. George received an offer to perform as an artist, guaranteeing $1,500 a week (to a preacher who made $150 a week). It wasn't even tempting. He laughed it off.

George and another evangelist had crusades in Lexington, Kentucky, at the same time and saw each other in a restaurant late at night. The other carried a bowling bag. "What do you have in there?" George asked with a smile.

"I've got the loot."

"What do you mean?"

"I count the offering and take the loose cash and change. Don't you?"

George says he kept as far away from that type as he could. "The rank and file were good men, but there were always a few who gave evangelists a bad name."

George ran into big-name stars like Mickey Mantle and Rosemary Clooney. After a meeting in Miami, George and Harold were— as usual—too keyed up to go to sleep right away. "Let's go to someplace famous for dessert," Harold suggested.

"Like where?"

"The Eden Rock Hotel."

"The Eden Rock? You think they'll let us get away with spending a total of five bucks between us?"

"Sure, this time of night we can just order sundaes." So, they went to the Eden Rock and sat there, George says, pretending to be important while waiting for their order, when a tall, slim, dynamic-looking black man slid into the booth next to theirs. Without hesitating, George walked over and sat next to him.

"I'm George Sweeting, an evangelist, and you're Nat King Cole."

Cole smiled and shook George's hand. "Yeah. That's right."

George told him where he was holding meetings. "Love to have you come. It would be an honor."

"I appreciate it. My daddy is a preacher. Preached in Birmingham, and now he's in Philly."

George shared what Christ had meant in his life. "Do you know the Lord, Mr. Cole?"

Cole nodded. "Yeah. I'm away from Him right now, but I know Him. Known Him all my life. Had a wonderful time with Him, too."

"I hope you can come out one night this week."

"You never know, Reverend Sweeting. I just might." But as far as George knows, he didn't. And George never saw him again. The most famous person George met was at 10 Downing Street in London. He just wanted to get a peek at where the prime minister lived when who should step out the door but Winston Churchill himself. George was wearing a very American, wide-brimmed hat. Churchill took one look at it and said, "You're American."

"Yes, sir."

Churchill was most hospitable, and George got the impression that he deeply appreciated America just then. The prime minister spent about fifteen minutes chatting and seemed pleased at George's complimenting him as an orator and quoting from his many classic speeches. George told him he was in London preaching at Royal Albert Hall, and Churchill wished him the best.

By the end of the fifties, George Sweeting was one of the busiest evangelists in America. He was preaching virtually every day, and when he took self-imposed breaks, he wrote more books. Oddly, despite the tension-related maladies, he did not feel burned out, exhausted, discouraged, or ready for a break. He wasn't looking into any other line of work, wasn't ready to make the transition into another field. He was productive and happy, and though he could have wished for more time at home with Hilda and the boys (there were four now, Robert Bruce having come along in 1959), he still thought he would travel and preach the rest of his life. He couldn't imagine any other ministry that would allow him to do what he loved best, preaching as often as possible.

By 1960, however, George sensed the need to be home more. Raising four boys was a big job for two people, but for a mother alone much of the time, it was especially tough. In George David, their eldest, George and Hilda had noticed a greater spirit of independence than in the other three. Young George himself admits this and points to it as a reason that he believes he didn't accept Christ as his Savior until he was in his thirties. In discussing what mistakes the elder Sweeting might have made with his son, young George says, "He really didn't. I was just a rascal, that's all. There wasn't anything he could or should have done differently. I had to learn the hard way, and his constant love and concern and prayer for me over the years has paid off."

In 1960 and early 1961, realizing he needed to be home more, George accepted campaigns primarily in New York, Philadelphia, Connecticut, and New Jersey. Though they were far apart, they were only two-and-one-half to three hours driving time from Wyckoff, and so George came home every night. It wasn't easy, but he felt it was the only way. "I felt I had been winning everybody else's kids to the Lord, and I didn't want to lose any of my own." By driving home late every night after the meetings, George was able to be up for breakfast with the kids the next morning and frequently drive them to school.

In God's timing, several churches simultaneously expressed an interest in having George serve as their senior pastor. A Pennsylvania church of nearly two thousand was one, and an Illinois church of more than seven hundred was another. Yet George chose a church of 150. Why? It was an inner-city church. It had seen great days, with an attendance of more than a thousand, so that would be a challenge. It was close enough so that he wouldn't have to move the family from their home in Wyckoff. The children wouldn't have to change schools. They wouldn't have to live in a fishbowl of a parsonage and have to deal with the preacher's kids syndrome. Also, the church building was within ten miles of Herrmann Braunlin's Hawthorne Gospel Church.

And the name of it just happened to be the Madison Avenue Baptist Church of Paterson.

14

The Miracle at Madison Avenue

eorge's earliest recollection of the Madison Avenue Baptist
Church was when his father took the family there when George
was a child. Rev. Edward Drew, the vibrant pastor then, was the
one who had assigned Herrmann Braunlin to pastor the Hawthorne
Gospel Church—an assignment that was to last sixty-two years. (In
fact, when Braunlin first went to Hawthorne, he was a layman who
was going to lead the meetings until the congregation could secure a
pastor.)

While Braunlin was settling in for the decades of faithful service
at Hawthorne, after twenty-eight years, Edward Drew moved on
from Madison Avenue and was replaced. The first successor may
have been threatened by the memory of such a powerful predecessor,
and so he quickly started doing away with some elements that were
tied to the man. The church had been known as a missionary
church—in fact, as mentioned previously, the Hawthorne Gospel
Church itself had been a missionary effort begun by Madison Avenue
Baptist.

But one of the succeeding pastors went so far as to take down the
missionary map in the foyer that had highlighted where the church's

missionaries were serving. He said, in effect, "The past is great, but we are no longer living in the past. We are looking to the future." But the map was not taken away. It was simply leaning against a back wall, where it reminded some of the faithful of the good days with Pastor Drew. Perhaps the new pastor might have been able to survive the psychologically bad idea of ridding the church of its heritage if he had not left elements of it in plain sight.

Regardless, the church lost many members under Edward Drew's successors, and by the time George Sweeting arrived on the scene, the church had dwindled to a shell of its former self. What was left from the glory days of a congregation of more than a thousand were just the 150 or so standbys who remembered the church when it was glorious, spirited, and vigorous. There were people there who had been saved under Pastor Drew and who had come out of all kinds of darkness because of him.

When George took over he didn't say anything. He simply acted. As a lover of history, a believer in the value of a sound heritage, he asked a woman in the church—an artist—to render a portrait of Edward Drew. As soon as it was available, he hung it in a prominent corner of the church. It spoke volumes, and the new man was accepted as a young pioneer who knew better than to forget the past. He studied the history of Edward Drew's pastorate there. He knew the man to have been a great Bible expositor. George tried to relate the past to the opportunities of the present and the future. He worked at knowing the people and listening to them. He was a home-going pastor. Every week he was in homes, winning people to Christ, praying with parishioners, facing their needs with them, letting them know he was one of them.

One of the first things George had to do from an administrative standpoint was to see that the neighborhood was somehow upgraded. The area had deteriorated to the point that it suffered from vandalism, inadequate lighting, and an occasional liquor bottle thrown from a passing car into the church's shrubs. He went to the city fathers and bargained with them. "If you can install lighting in our neighborhood, we'll start buying up some of the old homes, demolishing them, and creating off-street parking.

Then we'll upgrade our facility and make it a centerpiece for a renovated neighborhood."

The city reacted warmly, as did the congregation. Powerful streetlights were erected that drove some of the base element from the area and cut down on the danger and the vandalism. The church made good on its promise, and after buying and leveling several run-down houses, created enough off-street parking to handle much bigger crowds.

Meanwhile, George brought a combination of solid exposition and warm evangelism to the church, and it saw scores of new converts. Fresh life and enthusiasm were breathed into the congregation, and when the renovation and building program began, they were proud of their facility, their parking, their location, their pastor, and their potential. They invited many new families, and in a matter of four years, attendance was pushing eight hundred again. The evening service—in those days the harbinger of a growing church—often outstripped the morning worship service in attendance.

George took Mondays off, but a typical weekday in the Sweeting household saw George and Hilda rising early. George put Scottish marching band or Sousa records on the stereo and cranked up the volume, then went from door to door of his sons' bedrooms and roused them with a cheerful, "C'mon, guys, let's go." The boys remember that fondly, and some say they'll likely do the same with their children.

Dad had breakfast with the family and either saw them off or took them to school. Then he spent some leisurely moments with Hilda, chatting, strolling in the yard and the garden. Both have always enjoyed working with the soil, finding it therapeutic and tension-reducing. They discussed the children and any difficult relationship problems from the church only when the boys were not around. "We wanted to insure that their church memories were happy ones," George says, "so unless the problem was health-related and they could join us in prayer, we kept petty differences and conflicts from them."

Semiannually, George took each boy out to breakfast alone, let him order whatever he wanted, and then just let him talk for an hour or so. It was just a get-acquainted time, to find out where he was in his life and what he was thinking about, worrying about, praying about. Anything he wanted to tell his dad or ask him was fair game.

For years George added five dollars to the boys' savings accounts for each book they read and outlined for him. He suggested the titles, and when he approved the outline he added the money to their accounts. He encouraged all to read D. L. Moody's biography. Among other titles he suggested were Hudson Taylor's *Spiritual Secret,* Carnegie's *How to Win Friends and Influence People,* John Haggai's *How to Win over Worry,* J. Oswald Sanders's *Spiritual Leadership,* and, ironically, Norman Vincent Peale's *The Power of Positive Thinking.* George explains that even though sections of Peale's bestseller should be read with selectivity, he still felt it was a worthwhile book for his sons to read.

He also took the boys to professional ball games in New York, to the rodeo, and to such special attractions as the Ice Capades. For forty-five years the Sweetings have had three major picnics every year: Memorial Day, the Fourth of July, and Labor Day. Relatives or friends are invited, and now the boys bring their wives and children to the outings.

One day a week George took Hilda to lunch. "All the time," he says, "no matter what the circumstances. Sometimes on my day off, sometimes Friday, but we always did it." Then George was off to the office by 9:30 A.M. and spent the morning in study, sermon preparation, and handling correspondence. He generally had lunch at the office or out, then spent the afternoon in counseling or visitation. He would be home by 5:30 for dinner and family activities, whether it was attending kids' ball games or playing with them. "We played catch, we hit fly balls, we played pool or table tennis in the cellar or horseshoes outside. It was the exception if we were not competing in some sport nearly every day."

Then the kids did their homework. If George had a board meeting, he frequently stipulated at the beginning when it would end. Ten o'clock was a very late exception. One night he brought in a huge machete and laid it on the table. "Tonight, gentlemen, we're going to have a harmonious, short meeting." The men howled.

It was rare that there was a tense meeting at Madison Avenue, because it was George's experience that where there's blessing and growth, people are excited and eager to work together. Tuesday night was visitation night, and George always led these himself, partly to become an example but also because evangelism was his heartbeat. Wednesday night was prayer meeting and children's clubs, along with choir practice. Thursday nights and Friday nights were kept open so no one would be working in the church every night, although the church softball or basketball teams might schedule a game on those nights.

Youth socials were usually held on Saturdays, and the Sweetings frequently hosted seventy-five to one hundred teens. They provided games and food and a devotional time.

On Tuesday, November 2, 1965, the *Paterson Evening News* ran a huge, photo-filled feature entitled "New Madison Avenue Baptist Church Testimonial of Congregation's Faith in Future of City":

PATERSON—Five years ago the Madison Avenue Baptist Church felt the pinch of a declining congregation. The big question was to move or not to move. The suburbs or the city? After much soul searching, the church decided to remain at 900 Madison Avenue, where it has ministered for over seventy years. The men of the church decided to launch their own urban development. The first step was interior renovation involving thousands of dollars worth of volunteer labor. This has resulted in a beautiful, inviting sanctuary.

The next step was a badly needed face-lifting on the exterior which was completed three years ago under the direction of one of the members, George Mak. The elders and deacons believe that parking and adequate lighting are as necessary as pews and hymn books in this automobile age. Thus a detailed plan was inaugurated to secure off the street parking at the expense of buying adjacent homes. This ambitious plan has met with notable success, and the parking situation is greatly improved.

The declining congregation, armed with faith, prayer, and hard work, has shared its truth until empty pews are now full once again. In fact, last year all past records were broken, and 1965 is already surpassing 1964.

Last year the elders, deacons, and congregation agreed to expand and erect a three story educational building to care for the ever growing congregation. Money is always a problem, and so as a team, the men decided to do much of the building themselves. The steel was designed, ordered, fabricated, and for the most part, erected by the congregation. . . . The lower level will make room for 250 additional children. The street level includes a spacious foyer with modern rest rooms, library, a full gymnasium, and modern kitchen. The mezzanine includes the latest in nursery planning with three divisions. . . . The entire building is air conditioned.

The congregation has expressed gratitude to the Board of Education, Mayor Graves, and local business concerns for cooperation in this venture. The changes at Madison Avenue and Cedar Streets are quite miraculous: a timely tribute by a dedicated congregation to God, and the spiritual needs of Paterson. . . . Pastor George Sweeting declares, "Every problem is an opportunity to display God's power. No church has to die!"

Highlights from an editorial, "A True Example of Renewal," which appeared later on in the same newspaper:

Madison Avenue Baptist Church of Paterson is a refreshing example of good citizenship which thousands of others in the city could well emulate.

In The News tonight is an illustrated story of a do-it-yourself renewal project which should quicken the heartbeats of its pastor, the Rev. George Sweeting, and the members of the congregation and better the city-at-large.

[In the face of the church's problem five years ago], there was no bemoaning fate, no anguished resignation to an inevitable [end] that never came. The members pitched in with vigor and dedication and have now wrought a community wonder. . . .

Madison Avenue Baptist has indeed offered a challenge to the city as a whole, to its officials and its people, to adopt the same attitude of self-sacrifice as contrasted with others who are waiting for a federal handout to help them achieve what they could do for themselves in the old-time American spirit.

We salute the Rev. Sweeting and the members of the congregation for their hardy spirit and for their fine example.

What neither George nor Hilda Sweeting knew, however, was that the pastorate at Madison Avenue was preparatory for a similar task, on an even larger scale. Neither thought they would ever leave New Jersey. George was fascinated by the state and always had been. He and his wife loved the ocean, almost inordinately he says now. They found it therapeutic. "Whenever we would get overwhelmed, when we'd been going too hard or fast or long or there had been a crushing death, an emotional blow, a setback, we'd try to take a day and drive two hours to the ocean. Then we'd walk the beach, breathe in the salt air, listen to the gulls, watch the huge waves crash and the foam spray everywhere. The waves would roll up and wash our footprints away, reminding us how great was God's power and how frail we were. It gave us an eternal perspective. Then we'd enjoy a fish dinner and head back home refreshed, recharged, ready to get back at the task."

Other churches tried to lure George away, some from as far away as California. "We have the ocean out here, too, you know," they'd tell him. But he wasn't interested.

George turned forty-one in 1965. Hilda was thirty-nine. Their family was growing up. "We never intended to leave New Jersey."

15

Decisions, Decisions

eorge Sweeting had spoken at Moody Week in Winona Lake, Indiana, about every other year during the 1950s, but he was particularly pleased to be invited to Founder's Week in Chicago for the first time in February of 1965. He didn't realize that his ministry there attracted the attention of some lifetime members of the Moody Memorial Church, a mile north of the Institute. (Though the church and the Institute have common roots and are very close in doctrine and practice, they are entirely separate organizations.)

Moody Church had been without a senior pastor since 1962 when Alan Redpath left, and the historic body and facility were suffering. The cavernous sanctuary, which held forty-two hundred, echoed with some five hundred survivors scattered throughout the auditorium. The once grand church building showed neglect and lack of funds. The people were very much in need of a pastor but sensed that few quality men would be interested in the challenge of an inner-city church with an old facility in a difficult neighborhood, limited parking, and a dwindling congregation. Sound familiar?

In the fall of 1965, George held a united evangelistic crusade in a high school in St. Joseph, Michigan, unaware that the same people from Moody Church who had been impressed with him at Founder's Week were also in the audience. They were good meetings. The crowd built every night, people were enthusiastic, and many were converted. Unknown to George, members of the Moody Church pulpit committee were assigned to visit the Madison Avenue Baptist Church. If George was aware there were out-of-town visitors, he did not guess they were from Chicago or that they were part of a search committee.

He was invited to speak at Moody Church. He loved Chicago, the Institute, and Moody Church, so he was pleased to find an opening in his schedule. Hilda was a little wary of the invitation. "You know every time you speak at a church without a pastor, they wind up pursuing you."

"Oh, you don't have to worry about this one," he assured her. "I have no interest in pastoring Moody Church, let alone uprooting the family and leaving New Jersey. They want me to meet with the elder board in the afternoon, but just to brainstorm about their situation."

Both George's and Hilda's mothers were widows by then, and the Sweetings helped them with their yards and storm windows and kept an eye on them. George and Hilda had brothers and sisters within driving distance, too, and all the cousins got along well together. Young George had just begun his senior year of high school, and their youngest, Bob, was six. New Jersey was home, and that was that. George wanted to stay at Madison Avenue Baptist for his lifetime ministry.

After the service in Chicago, the elders asked George what he felt was the answer to an inner-city church like theirs. "What would justify their geographic location?"

Not candidating and totally unaware of their interest in him, he was blunt. Those at that meeting recall that he recommended a combination of Bible teaching and evangelism. "The old-timers are dying, and the young couples are moving to the suburbs for better school systems, so you have to be winning them faster than you're losing them. You should look at your church as a mission station open to all people. It needs a creative, flexible program. We've found that what pews are to the normal church, a parking lot is to a city church. You have to do something about the parking."

He also recommended fortifying the evening service with youth groups, adult Bible classes, training sessions, even a dinner to get families to come and then stay for the evening service. Following the service, he said, involve your college and career and singles groups in their activities. "Think about a day-care center. Justify your existence in the neighborhood by serving the people who live *here*. Then you can reach the parents for Christ and minister to them.

"Try a direct-mail program into these high-rises. People of all economic levels are shut up there, and no one is allowed to visit them. If you can get some of them interested, maybe you can get some members in there for Bible studies."

When they put a direct question to him, George answered straight on. "What do you think of this church?"

"Clearly, sadly, it appears to be dying. I hate to say this, but there's not a lot that the regenerate would be attracted to, let alone the unregenerate. You need an exciting team, a flexible program, know your constituency, find out where your people live."

"Could you do that here, Rev. Sweeting? Could you assemble an attractive team and make this work relevant?"

George was stunned. "Oh, no, I'm not your man. I'm just here as a friend, a consultant shooting from the hip. If I were candidating, I would not have rambled on or been so blunt."

In the end they urged him to at least think and pray about it. He agreed he would do that, but he really didn't foresee anything coming of it. He hadn't even admitted the possibility of his interest to himself, but Hilda saw a spark of it when he returned. "You're not interested, are you?" she said.

"No, I don't think so. I'll go back and preach for them again, but I can't see it."

In November 1965, the church asked him to bring Hilda with him to a Wednesday night service. By then, George was starting to see the challenge. Hilda was still closed to the idea and was uneasy that the church had a receiving line for them, "as if we had already decided to come. And we hadn't. At least I'm sure I hadn't." George tried to excite her with the vibrancy of the city of Chicago, and short of that, he asked her to pray about it. During their devotional times together, he said, they should write out the pros and cons of such a move.

Still, even George wasn't sure. Those who knew about Moody Church's interest in him advised him not to consider it. "It's a blimp hangar," one said. "They're going to sell it one day for a roller rink."

Someone else said, "What do you think you can do with a church like that? You're a chalk artist." There's always someone available to keep you humble. In fact, by then George had virtually given up chalk drawing, because even though it was effective, he felt the need to major on the majors and not to detract from the preaching of the Word. Regardless, the comment stung, as do such shots as, "Sweeting is OK, but he's pompous," which he's heard over the years. People who know him know such epithets are untrue, yet they cause George to look up and say, "Lord, help me."

Asked to speak at Moody Founder's Week again in February of 1966, George was by then carefully considering the Moody Church pastorate, but he tended to agree with his wife that the move didn't seem right for the family. It would be disruptive to the boys' school years, and there were too many other reasons to stay in New Jersey. The only person who believed George should accept the challenge was Herrmann Braunlin, a man too deep and impressive to ignore.

The month after Founder's Week '66, George was down with the flu. A friend who should have known better took a verse from Psalm 23 out of context and speculated to him that God "made you lie down, so you can really think about this." Despite the liberty the man had taken with the Scripture, George got the legal pad out again and began seriously considering his decision. The Moody Church people held the position open for him, and for some reason, he had not turned it down yet.

Meanwhile, Hilda was going through her own struggle, and she knew that George would not proceed—or would at least give the decision even more time—if she could not obtain peace about the possibility. She saw things moving toward the direction of Chicago, and she got serious about seeking God on the matter. George was on the road shortly after that when she finally was able to tell the Lord that she would be willing to go, if that's what He directed. George called and said, "Honey, I feel that we're to go to Moody Church. If you still feel strongly, I'll wait, but I feel it's right."

"I'm willing, but I *am* concerned for the boys because George is a senior, and it'll be a traumatic move for all of us."

"I'll just tell them I can't come until August 1. George will have graduated, and the kids will be out of school. And that'll give Madison Avenue plenty of notice."

The week before, George had been having breakfast with a neighboring pastor who mentioned that he had heard that "Moody Church is interested in you."

"Yeah," George had said, "but I don't think I'm going."

"Yes, you are. I can see it in your eyes."

"No, I really don't think I am."

In the meantime, George and Hilda had decided to accept and informed Moody Church of the only acceptable timetable. George asked them to keep it confidential because he felt it was too early to make such an announcement at his own church. The following Sunday afternoon, with George on his way back from Chicago, the Sweeting phone was busy. People from Madison Avenue Baptist told Hilda they were hearing from parishioners in a neighboring church that their pastor had said George Sweeting was going to be the next pastor of Moody Church in Chicago. Hilda was upset. She asked what exactly had been said. Apparently, the pastor was guessing, based on what he thought he had seen in George's eyes at breakfast, and in an offhanded comment in his sermon mentioned that he had recently spoken with "Rev. Sweeting, whom I believe may be the next pastor of Moody Church." The word spread like wildfire.

Hilda called the offending pastor. "It may have been because I was only resigned to the move and not certain about it," she recalls, "but I told him clearly that I thought he was off base with such a comment when we hadn't even announced it to our people yet. He apologized to me and later to George. But it was an unfortunate way to have it announced to the people at Madison Avenue Baptist."

That summer the Sweetings moved to Deerfield, Illinois, where the boys could have a little running room. The move was hard on Hilda, and the worst snowstorm in Chicago history the following January didn't help. That spring Deerfield was flooded, and they had a foot of water in their basement. A nearby town was hit by a tornado. "I have to admit there were times when I questioned the move and wanted to go home," Hilda says. "I was frankly a little bit afraid of a big-city church. I'm a person who's more comfortable in a smaller church."

There were reasons to be afraid of a city church. More than once, George heard gunfire as he passed the Cabrini Green housing projects on Division Street. "I put the visor down to at least have some protection," he says. "I doubt it would have deflected a bullet."

George emphasized the open-door nature of the church by always welcoming the poor and outcast, but sometimes a fringe element also attended the services. One deranged man had been bothering some of the women, so George and his new youth pastor, Jim Gwinn—who was to become a close friend of more than twenty years—asked the man not to return. He was a big, strong man who had single-handedly rescued someone from drowning in the Chicago River, so when he asked Gwinn if he wanted to "settle this in Lincoln Park," Gwinn said, "Not on your life." The man continued to attend.

During a church picnic football game, George tackled the man so enthusiastically that he developed a new respect, and fear, for the pastor. Once George held the man's necktie gently and reminded him with a smile that if he got out of line, "I'll give you one right to the jaw."

By the time Campus Crusade for Christ founder and president Bill Bright came in for a five-day lay crusade on evangelism, the man had been barred from the church. He came in anyway, while Bright was speaking on the floor in front of the pulpit. The man went up on the podium, wrapped his arms around the huge, old pulpit, and rocked it till it broke off its supports and crashed down, missing Bright by a foot. After that the man was banned from the church by court order.

When George had Jim Voss, a former criminal, in to speak, he let him use his study while George handled a baptismal service. While baptizing someone, George thought he saw policemen with drawn weapons jogging up the side aisles toward the steps that led to his office. *I must be working too hard,* he told himself. *I'm seeing things.* When Voss came down to speak after the song service, he told the congregation that he worked in New York's Hell's Kitchen, and that he appreciated Rev. Sweeting making him feel at home. He said he had seen a man with a butcher knife on the roof outside the office window and called the police. They were there within minutes. The man had escaped from a local halfway house, one of dozens in the area, and the police finally apprehended him in the church's Philpott Hall.

When the Democratic National Convention was held in Chicago in 1968 and the hippies congregated at Lincoln Park across from the church, a few dozen of them showed up for services. George told the congregation to accept them as they would anyone else and not to react, no matter what they said or did. When the demonstrators eventually marched down LaSalle Street, breaking windows and blocking traffic, they did no damage to either Moody Church or the Moody Bible Institute. A young demonstrator was shot on the steps at Moody Church, however, when he pulled a knife on a policeman.

Some early meetings with Jack Wyrtzen filled Moody Church four times in a row, and George was off and running with the biggest challenge of his life. "I got a map of Chicago and located with pins every member in the city and the suburbs." Using different colors, he plotted prospective members, starting with the relatives of members and regular attenders. One Sunday morning he gave everyone a card and preached on the theme that when Zion travails, she brings forth children. He asked the people to prayerfully list those individuals they were burdened for within a fifty-mile radius of the church. Two weeks later, he initiated a program in which every prospect was visited.

George preached evangelistically almost every Sunday night. It was rare when he didn't give an invitation, and even rarer that many didn't respond. "It was easy to direct them to the counseling rooms, which were through doors on either side of the platform. Trained counselors went with them and dealt with them privately. New converts were put in a thirteen-week orientation class, then into a thirteen-week discipleship class, both of which I taught until I found someone who could take them over. Before we would take new converts into membership, they knew what they believed and where we stood, and why. They had to come for twenty-six weeks, so if they weren't going to follow through, we found out soon enough. Then we integrated them into a class in the regular Sunday school."

The proven strategy had the blessing of God, and Moody Church was coming back to life. Moody students came by the score. Even the president of Moody, Dr. William Culbertson, was a regular Sunday morning attender beginning in 1968. He asked George to serve on the board of trustees as the alumni representative in April 1969. It was a high honor and a rare treat for George, but occasionally a friend or an associate would make too much of it.

"Someday you're going to be president of that place," one said.

"It was so silly," George recalls. "I told 'em, 'You're out of your mind.' I loved pastoring the Moody Church."

16

The Big One

When George Sweeting left New Jersey to become pastor of the Moody Memorial Church in Chicago, a few friends predicted that he would one day become president of the Moody Bible Institute. He knew they probably didn't even realize that the institutions were not officially associated with each other, and he had never considered himself an educator anyway, so he didn't give much thought to the comments.

It wasn't that he didn't have the intelligence to be comfortable in an academic environment. When he had attended the Art Institute in Chicago, he also enrolled at Northern Baptist Theological Seminary and took the four hardest professors he could find. His brother Bill had told him about the Harold Lindsells and the Carl F. H. Henrys and had warned him that he wouldn't get one A. George got no lower than a 95 percent in all of the four courses. But both his brothers had gone on to earn doctorates, and though George would one day be awarded four honorary doctorates and offered others, he felt inadequate when people mentioned his name in connection with an educational institution.

In 1969, his alma mater, Gordon College, queried his interest in

being a candidate for their presidency. He assured them he was flattered by their interest but insisted that he didn't feel he would be right
for a liberal arts setting. They would be broader than he would have
felt comfortable with, but still they wanted to fly him and Hilda out to
chat. "Are you sure you want to go to that expense when I'm certain
I'm not your man?" They were.

He and Hilda enjoyed their time there and received a beautiful
rocking chair with the college logo on it. George was named alumnus
of the year and was awarded his first honorary doctorate, from Gordon Conwell Seminary. During the discussion, when it simply
became clear in George's mind that he would not be the right choice,
he made a statement that he intended to be taken at face value at the
time, but of which he was later reminded. He said, "Although I don't
believe a liberal arts college is right for me, the day may come that if I
were given the opportunity to head up a Bible college where they
were training people exclusively to be pastors, evangelists, missionaries, and Christian communicators, I might be interested in that." He
was not thinking of the Moody Bible Institute. In fact, he says, if he
was thinking of anything, it was a small Bible college.

So when a couple of his fellow Moody trustees started making
noises in 1970 that he might be a candidate to replace Dr. Culbertson,
George hardly gave it a thought. He assumed that the trustees who
mentioned the presidency to him were acting independently and were
just starting a long-term search with the first name they could think
of.

But when such things are being discussed in private at high levels, they have a way of getting out via the grapevine and rumor mills.
Dr. Sweeting didn't know it, but not only were a couple of trustees
interested in his candidacy, so was Dr. Culbertson.

When the discussions came up at the trustee board meeting, Dr.
Sweeting recommended Dr. Robert A. Cook of the King's College in
Briarcliff Manor, New York. But Dr. Cook was in his fifties by then,
and the board was looking for a man in his forties. A few other names
were talked about, but no conclusions were drawn.

The next week, the chairman of the board met with George. "Dr.

Sweeting, the majority of the men on the board feel that you're the man."

"Oh, I'm flattered," George said, "but I'm so unlike Dr. Culbertson. I've been an evangelist and a pastor, but . . ."

"These men have done their homework, George. They feel this very deeply."

"Well, I appreciate that, but I just don't see it."

Shortly thereafter, Jim Gwinn, Dr. Sweeting's youth man at Moody Church, announced that he was leaving to become director of the Lake Sammamish Bible Conference Center, east of Seattle. In probing to see if his good friend had any problems at Moody Church or with him, Dr. Sweeting reminded Jim that he had been with Moody Church less than three years.

"Well, you're going to become president of the Moody Bible Institute and leave me here, and I don't want to be here without you."

"Jim, that's ridiculous. I do not intend to go to Moody Bible Institute."

George really thought that was the end of the pressure to get him to consider the job, so when Dr. Culbertson asked to meet him for lunch at the Union League Club of Chicago in November 1970, he assumed they would be chatting about other names. He had heard that Dr. David Gotaas, head of the missions department at Moody (who would later become pastor of the Winnetka Bible Church), was under consideration. "I'm relieved," he told Hilda. Maxwell Coder, vice president and dean of education, had twice asked him to speak to the faculty. Both times he found it difficult to look out at the faces of his former teachers and a score of others who had more education than he. "The job scares me to death," he told his wife. "I hope they go with Dr. Cook or Dr. Gotaas or someone else."

Hilda often told him that she didn't know what came over him when he spoke in a Moody Bible Institute setting. "It's as if you freeze up for some reason," she said. "Anywhere else, you cut loose and preach the way you've been gifted to preach." They agreed that something at Moody intimidated him.

After lunch at the Union League Club with Dr. Culbertson, the older man slid his chair back and spoke softly. He was never a dramatic man, so his approach was a surprise. "George, it was at this table many years ago that Will Houghton spoke to me about becoming president of the Moody Bible Institute."

Uh-oh, Dr. Sweeting thought, *here it comes.* His heart almost stopped.

Dr. Culbertson told him that he had been observing him for years as a student, as an evangelist, as a pastor, and most recently as his own pastor and as a trustee. "You have judgment," he said. "Wisdom beyond your years. I've given it a lot of thought and prayer, George, so I don't want you to pass this off lightly. I believe you are the man God would have as the next president of Moody Bible Institute."

Even as he thought of his objections, something had pierced George Sweeting's heart. If William Culbertson, a man of God, a man of deep prayer, was convinced that he was the one, perhaps it was possible. But how?

"Dr. Culbertson, I'm deeply humbled. I'm honored. I'm flattered. But I don't think I'm your man. I have little experience with a school."

"George, you've taught evangelism for us. I know you taught evening school in your home church in New Jersey. You've been a teaching pastor."

"But I'm not an academic man. I'm primarily a pastor with an evangelist's heart."

"George, if you'll notice the rhythm of the Moody Bible Institute, you'll know we were founded by an evangelist. D. L. Moody was succeeded by R. A. Torrey, another evangelist. Then we had James M. Gray, an administrator/educator, then Houghton, a promoter pastor. We need now the gifts that you have." He looked deep into George's eyes. "I'm convinced you're the man."

George was speechless. The president had heard his arguments and was ready for them. George was sure he was not right for the job; Culbertson believed that a necessity to depend solely upon God was a prerequisite. "Will you at least think and pray about it and discuss it with your wife?"

"I will."

"And when might I expect your decision?"

George thought. He had never made snap decisions. He wanted to be as sure of this as Dr. Culbertson was. "I'd like ninety days," he said.

Culbertson pressed his lips together. "Very well," he said. "That will allow me to make the announcement at Founder's Week in February."

George and Hilda talked about it and prayed about it every day during those three months. They found themselves excited over the possibilities. George couldn't shake the feeling that if God had impressed him upon Dr. Culbertson's heart and mind, he shouldn't discount it. But he wanted the same peace about the decision. Hilda felt honored that he had been asked, and she appreciated Dr. Culbertson's opinion of her husband. But she loved the pastorate, loved having a church base. She would be willing to support George, whatever his decision.

As Founder's Week approached, Dr. Culbertson approached George. "Do you have an answer for me?"

"I don't. I would like to ask for another ninety days."

Culbertson was disappointed but agreed to the extension. He reminded George that he would be away for three weeks following Founder's Week, relaxing and regrouping and speaking occasionally at Southern Keswick and in other Florida locations.

While he was away George and Hilda came to their decision. "I didn't feel qualified," he recalls, "and I suppose I would have been more scared if I had. No one should come into a responsibility like that one feeling as if he is perfectly capable in himself. I knew better. I knew the only way it would work would be with my total dependence upon God. I knew the Institute had influence and a great reputation, but I didn't know how much or how wide it was until I was in the job. If I had known, I might not have taken it."

George communicated his decision to a jubilant Culbertson and asked for a starting date of August 1, 1971. He assured the family that they would continue to attend Moody Church until the children were out of high school. He didn't want to disrupt their friendships and attachments. It may not have been the best thing to do to his successor; sometimes it's difficult to have the previous pastor remain in the church. But it worked well, and the new man insisted that he had no problem with it.

George was deeply concerned that Moody Church not have to go through what they had gone through before he came. He didn't want to see the place flounder for years without a senior pastor. He recommended to the board two men, Dave Burnham and Warren Wiersbe, as initial prospects. Burnham's church was in the middle of a building project, and he felt it was the wrong time. Dr. Wiersbe, of Calvary Baptist in Covington, Kentucky, was open to candidating. Dr. Sweeting had heard him many times in different settings and had him in as a guest at Moody Church. George was impressed, and the congregation responded well.

The elders visited Dr. Wiersbe's church and liked what they saw. After he candidated the Moody Church congregation was excited. Dr. Sweeting chaired the meeting when the vote was taken and the call extended. George agreed to finish on a Wednesday night in August, even after he had officially begun at the Institute, with Pastor Wiersbe taking over the following Sunday. "It was a marvelous transition," George says. "It transpired without a ripple, and the church never missed a beat. Dr. Wiersbe served effectively and successfully and was a marvelously gifted pastor."

Chicago still had four daily newspapers in 1971—the *Tribune,* the *Sun-Times,* the *Daily News,* and the *Today*—and all four covered the official installation of Dr. William Culbertson as chancellor and Dr. George Sweeting as the sixth president of the Moody Bible Institute on September 28, 1971. It ushered in sixteen of the most aggressive, ambitious, and progressive years since the founding of the Moody Bible Institute.

17

Into a New Century

r. Sweeting plunged into plans for growth. He challenged employees to dream dreams of what God might do through them and through the Institute. He and his associates immediately went to work on a fifteen-year plan that would culminate with the Institute's centennial in 1986.

A nationwide radio broadcast rested near the top of his priority list—one that would present the gospel and at the same time familiarize new people with Moody. He soon went on the air with a weekly half-hour program, *Moody Presents*, heard on several 50,000-watt secular stations and more than two hundred Christian stations.

With the 1972 Munich Olympics around the corner, the Institute sent fifty student counselors to Munich to join forces with the Moody Institute of Science in an outreach to the crowds. Thousands attended their daily film showings on Petershoff Square. Tragedy struck when terrorists stormed the quarters of Israeli athletes, but even that opened unexpected doors for the gospel.

Late in 1973, Dr. Sweeting and the Moody Chorale retraced the steps of Dwight L. Moody through his British Isles crusades exactly one hundred years earlier. In England, Scotland, and Ireland, they packed churches, school assemblies, and civic auditoriums. Dr. Sweeting addressed the political leaders of Scotland in several big cities.

The next three years students and employees turned to their own Jerusalem: Chicago itself. Using the medium of direct mail, a personal letter from Dr. Sweeting went to four hundred thousand homes on the city's north side. The letter outlined the plan of salvation and offered a free Moody correspondence lesson, *The Good Life*. In follow-up, staff and students called personally in many homes. A large rally climaxed the 1974 Chicago Evangelism Outreach. (Similar campaigns reached the west and south sides of the city in 1975 and 1976.) This effort resulted in hundreds of professions of faith.

A nationwide pastors' conference in 1973, also one of Dr. Sweeting's dreams, brought more than six hundred pastors to the campus from thirty-seven states, Puerto Rico, and Scotland. No more than three hundred had been anticipated. In following years, attendance spiraled to more than fifteen hundred. The annual event has sent thousands of pastors back to churches with new vision, enthusiasm, and spiritual commitment.

The education branch also moved ahead. The new advanced studies program brought college graduates to the campus for thirty hours of postbaccalaureate work in an intensive one-year study. University students took advantage of this program to ground themselves in the Scriptures en route to the mission field. He wanted to see enrollment in the day school increase from nine hundred to fourteen hundred in fifteen years—which it did during a period when most Christian colleges saw decreases in enrollment. By the end of Dr. Sweeting's presidency, a four-year baccalaureate was in place.

The Bible Lands Tour was initiated under Dr. Sweeting, as were the satellite evening schools, the master's degree program, and the push for accreditation, which was accomplished by the end of the eighties.

Enrollment in the Evening School climbed as the Institute planted evening extension schools in places like Joliet, Illinois, and Akron, Ohio. Radio also expanded in the early Sweeting years. The Institute opened WMBW in Chattanooga, KMBI AM-FM in Spokane,

WRMB in Boynton Beach, Florida, and WKES in St. Petersburg, Florida. That gave Moody eleven owned and operated stations in seven cities. And Moody programming could be heard in more than 290 locations via satellite.

Moody magazine more than doubled its circulation in the early seventies, climbing to a quarter-million subscribers. The Evangelical Press Association in 1976 named *Moody* magazine the most improved in its category, the best in its category, and the overall Periodical of the Year.

Moody Press, the book publishing operation that already had more than a thousand titles in its line, took a major step in these same years when it launched into Bible publishing, a considerable investment. It became a prime distributor of the *New American Standard Bible*, and soon to follow was the *Ryrie Study Bible*, a best-selling flagship product.

In 1973, as the new inner campus and plaza emerged, Chicago's Mayor Daley presented MBI a Chicago Beautiful Award in recognition of "significant contributions to beautification of the City."

The physical growth of the MBI campus is probably the most extraordinary accomplishment of the Sweeting years. This involved great vision, careful planning, and perseverance as Vice President Marvin Beckman negotiated seemingly endlessly with neighbors and city officials for property that has been valued in the millions of dollars. The campus grew from two city blocks to more than ten blocks, providing for future expansion.

As the nation geared up to celebrate its 1976 bicentennial, so did the Moody Bible Institute. A gigantic religious and patriotic rally in Chicago's Amphitheater on the closing Sunday afternoon of Founder's Week saw more than twelve thousand jam the stadium. Wesley Hartzell, reporter for the *Chicago Tribune,* called it an incredible event in an age when the words *God* and *patriot* were being scorned. Backdropped by a flag measuring forty by sixty feet and the massed banners of the fifty states, Dr. Sweeting warned that the nation was drifting away from God and the Bible, whose laws lay at the very roots of the country's founding.

"We of the Moody Bible Institute are not prophets of gloom and doom," he declared. "Neither are we gullible optimists. The nation could have no greater birthday gift than that the regular reading of the Bible be restored to the public schools."

Instead of the Bible, he observed, the nation is reading obscenity. "There are thirteen million filthy magazines sold each month. We protest them. Rome traveled this road and died. America is speeding along the same highway."

Dr. Sweeting called for renewal on three fronts:

To, first and foremost, Jesus Christ. To magnify righteousness and re-stigmatize sin.

To be the right kind of citizens—to be what Jesus called the salt and light of the earth.

To build healthy, good, moral, godly families.

"Patriotic music," wrote reporter Hartzell, "stirred long-forgotten scenes in the minds of older persons who may have remembered singing the great songs of America in Independence Day parades and rallies in the small towns where they grew up."

George W. Dunne, president of the Cook County board of commissioners, wrote later: "What a wonderful afternoon! I know that there will be many bicentennial activities throughout the year, but none will be more thrilling or inspirational than the affair at the Amphitheater."

In 1978, when a neo-Nazi group threatened to march in the heavily Jewish populated Chicago suburb of Skokie, Dr. Sweeting guided the Moody Bible Institute to run ads in both the *Chicago Tribune* and the *Chicago Sun-Times*, outlining its support for the people of Israel and its position against the march. In the open letter, the Institute pledged to stand with the Jewish community against propaganda of hatred. Dr. Sweeting was honored by leaders of the Jewish community and by a personal visit from Yitzhak Rabin of Israel.

Near the close of 1978 Dr. Sweeting announced as a goal for the coming year his reiterated pursuit of excellence. "To me excellence is a characteristic of God," he said. "The Scripture says His name is excellent. His loving-kindness is excellent, His salvation is excellent,

His way is excellent, His work is excellent, and His will is excellent. I look at excellence not as a fleshly characteristic at all but as a reflection of all that God is and all that He does and all that He represents." Excellence was the recurring theme of the Sweeting years.

In 1981, a surprise chapel honored Dr. Sweeting on his tenth anniversary as president. Many friends and relatives, including his wife and sons, Pastor Herrmann Braunlin, and others came to pay tribute. One of the highlights was a letter from Dr. Sweeting's sons, penned by Don. Here are excerpts from that letter:

Congratulations, Dad!

George, Jim, Bob, and I join with our friends at Moody in celebrating your 10th anniversary. Know that we are proud of you and love you very much. Know that we appreciate the heritage you've given . . . a heritage of faith and vision. We are with you after the meetings are over and see that you do live by God's Word and believe His promises....

You are an avid reader who applies what he reads and then passes a book on to others. In fact, you are the only father we know who would give his teenage sons good books to read and then promise to pay us for reading and outlining them. What motivation! But we learned. . . .

You wake up in the morning like a cannonball being fired. It got us moving! You love to laugh, and we like to see you laugh and relax.

We know that you were once told that you would probably never be able to have children. But today, the four of us salute you and thank God for His grace in giving you to us.

We look forward to your companionship in the years to come.

With deepest love and admiration,
George, Jim, Bob, and Don

As Dr. Sweeting succeeded Irwin Moon as the voice and figure of Moody Institute of Science films, his identity grew not only nationally but also abroad. Periodic trips to the mission fields of the world established him as an international figure. In 1983, for example,

Korean Christians invited him to help them celebrate the centennial of Protestant missionary influence in that land. His days there took him to some of Korea's largest evangelical churches, including the Young Nak Church in Seoul, which has sixty thousand members. Dr. Sweeting spoke at two of the five Sunday morning services and preached the gospel to thirty thousand people live and via closed circuit television. That same evening, he preached at the Kwang Lim Church in Seoul, which has twelve thousand members and three morning worship services. A church-growth seminar at Kwang Lim drew thousands of pastors.

The trip culminated with a four-evening evangelistic crusade in Inchon. A thousand people made decisions to receive Christ during the crusade.

George Sweeting is known around the world. For sixteen years he proved an invaluable asset to the Institute in his abilities as an orator, motivator, and administrator. Eager to share the spotlight, Dr. Sweeting praises his secretary, Betty McIntyre, as "proficient, capable, and trustworthy. Never once did she break a confidence."

The years of triumph, however, were not without their strain. Dr. Sweeting had his detractors. He firmly believes that no good is served by rehashing old debates or trying to prove irrelevant points. "You can't win when you defend yourself," he says. "If you convince someone that your opponent was wrong, it looks like the big institution picking on the little guy. If you don't convince anyone you were right, you're open to unconstructive criticism again."

Consistently, the record shows that George Sweeting was generous even to those with whom he felt it necessary to part company. They may have disagreed with him. They may have continued to attack him, but they were never able to say that he wasn't fair and generous, or that he either continued a fruitless argument or carried a grudge.

Why so generous, even to those that others might consider opponents? "I struggled so much as a child, picking beans until I could see them in my sleep. And then running milk from age eleven. I always worked and worked hard. I love to work, but the money came hard. When I was at Moody and working at the Baptista Film Company on Huron Street, I can remember trudging back to the Institute looking in the gutter all the way, hoping to find a dime so I could buy some lunch.

"I don't want to see anybody down and out if I can help it. I view generosity as an attribute of God that I want to reflect."

His tension-related chest pains returned and then dissipated by the early eighties. In 1984, during a routine prostate procedure, more cancerous cells were detected and required surgery, followed by thirty radiation treatments. More slowly than before, but completely nonetheless, Dr. Sweeting bounced back to full health, and by the last two years of his presidency, he was again active in sports with his grown sons and his grandchildren. He wanted to leave the presidency when he was healthy and still had many productive years ahead.

When he suggested to the board of trustees that a search begin for his successor, they at first rejected the idea and urged him to stay on until he was seventy. But, in fact, his fifteen-year plan was, from the beginning, his idea of the right tenure. He had wished to leave the job in 1986. He insisted that a search begin.

In February of that year he had Warren Wiersbe, Charles Swindoll, James Boice, Josh McDowell, and others at Founder's Week for the Centennial celebration. Billy Graham, Cliff Barrows, and George Beverly Shea—who served for eight years as a staff announcer at WMBI in Chicago in the thirties and forties—were featured at the closing rally, and more than seventeen thousand showed up at the Rosemont Horizon. Dr. Sweeting was criticized in some quarters for inviting Dr. Graham, but again, he refuses to defend the decision. Their roots are similar, and he had always admired Graham's boldness to preach the unadulterated gospel in any setting.

"Mr. Graham is to the twentieth century what D. L. Moody was to the nineteenth century," he says. "I have no doubt history will affirm this. He has preached to more people than any person in history, and the occasion at the Horizon was a historic event."

In July 1986, Dr. Sweeting was invited to speak at Amsterdam '86, the international meeting of itinerant evangelists, sponsored by the Graham organization. After a rousing address, Dr. Sweeting sat down on the platform. While someone was wrapping up the meeting, Dr. Graham passed George a note:

"Dear George, thank you for one of the greatest sermons I've ever heard. Thank you. Thank you. Love in Christ, Billy."

Later he received a letter from the evangelist. Some highlights:

My dear George,

If, as you said, the secret of the Christian life is a series of new beginnings—I think many of us made a new beginning after hearing your talk! What a tremendous thing it would be (again, as you said) if the commitment of 10,000 people in Amsterdam was so complete that we would make hell gasp for breath.

Your contribution was tremendous and made the evening a very special one. . . .

Hoping our paths will cross again soon. With warmest Christian greetings.

Cordially yours,
Billy

By the time he returned to the States, the matter of his replacement was moving quickly. He felt privileged to have been appointed to the search committee, and he was also pleased when their recommendation found unanimous and hearty support from the full board. In February 1987, the chairman of the board of trustees made the announcement after the last meeting of Founder's Week. George Sweeting would become the third chancellor of the Moody Bible Institute, and Joseph M. Stowell, the forty-three-year-old pastor of the Highland Park Baptist Church, Southfield, Michigan, would become the seventh president.

Dr. Sweeting was thrilled with the appointment and worked vigorously to lift up Dr. Stowell in his new position. Dr. Sweeting's goal was to energetically take up his new duties in representing the school, making calls on behalf of the Century II building program, writing, and preaching. The transition was harmonious, and Dr. Stowell seemed to enjoy his new role as much as Dr. Sweeting appreciated moving on to something fresh and innovative in his life.

Mr. Mitchell, chairman of the trustees, and Paul H. Johnson, the vice-chairman of the board, honored him with the following tributes:

Dear George:

You have provided for the future of MBI in a most effective way. God has given you wisdom and insight over the years to develop, expand and protect MBI, to administer its functions smoothly, and to provide an opportunity for the next generation of leadership.

On behalf of all of us, George, thank you for all you have done so well for the cause of the Gospel at MBI. May God be pleased to grant you many years of sweet fellowship, continued effective leadership at MBI and other places, broad influence through your speaking and writing, and the greatest fulfillment in your gift and calling in every way. The transition with Dr. Stowell seems to have been effective to its maximum, thanks to your generous attitude and efforts, and the future of the ministry of MBI owes much to this and to other decisions you have made. May God bless you in every way. It has been a blessing for me to have enjoyed our years of working together. Thank you for that as well.

Cordially in Christ,
William F. Mitchell, Sr.

Dear Dr. Sweeting:

I was just thinking about you and wondering what thoughts were going through your mind as you come to the final days of your sixteen years as president of Moody Bible Institute.

Certainly, you must have mixed feelings. Perhaps a little nostalgia as you look back over sixteen years of memories and the good times and the blessings the Lord has allowed you to enjoy as the head of one of the greatest institutions for the cause of Jesus Christ in the history of Christendom.

I would think you might also have a sense of relief that you won't have to carry the total burden of the day-to-day problems, pressures and activities that go with such a responsibility.

But I hope that the overriding and most significant feeling you have at this time is one of great satisfaction and delight in what has been accomplished and the lives you have influenced for the cause of Jesus Christ during your tenure as president. The Lord has allowed you not only to see the school remain faithful to its purposes and the Word of God, but also to grow in numbers and to set the wheels in motion for even greater growth into its second century, both academically and physically.

You must also feel very satisfied with your choice of Joe Stowell as the new president. It must give you a sense of comfort to know that the Institute will be in good hands and that you made a wise choice.

You must also feel good that you won't be leaving, but that you will still be able to use all of the experience and background in a positive way as you take on the new position as chancellor. What a nice arrangement to be able to be involved in the joys and blessings without all of the detail and responsibility....

You have been an inspiration to me and a role model to follow as to your personal walk with the Lord and Christian demeanor. You have always been a gentleman in every way, and you certainly exemplify the Fruit of the Spirit as well as anyone I know. I count it a privilege to be your friend.

My prayer for you these days is that you feel pleased, satisfied and comfortable with your life and what God has allowed you to see accomplished thus far for His glory.... I believe that's the way the Lord feels about you ... right about now ... very pleased, satisfied, and delighted.

> *Your friend in Christ,*
> *Paul H. Johnson*

Dr. Sweeting looked forward to a little more time at home, more time with his wife and grandchildren, and more time for his main loves: preaching and writing. "Sixteen years of administration is just about right," he says with a smile.

How does he assess himself? He doesn't think about self-assessment too much, he says, except for trying to continually examine himself in the light of Scripture. "I want to be obedient," he says. "I want to strive for excellence and to be a channel of God's love."

Some years before, in an assessment of evangelical leaders, a writer described Dr. Sweeting as an open fundamentalist. Though it may have been intended as a jab, Sweeting liked it. "I felt pretty good about it," he says. "I thought it was accurate. When it comes to preaching, I will preach anywhere in the world, if I have complete freedom to preach the gospel as I know it. My son Don says that 'precise doctrine, coupled with a narrow temperament, often results in a strict separatist, whereas precise doctrine coupled with an open temperament results in an open-minded fundamentalist.' Well, I like that, too. I am a fundamentalist in doctrine and an evangelical in spirit.

"My roots were in a warm, loving fundamentalist family and church. I memorized Scriptures from a Scofield Bible. My church was dynamic, thoughtful, sane, and fully committed to the Scriptures. Were there excesses? In my case, very few that I can remember. They gave me a reverence and love for the Scriptures. They encouraged a passion for the souls of all men, and I lift up my voice in praise and gratitude for their dedication. They taught me that 'living' meant 'giving.'"

And he seldom represses a generous impulse.

18

Chancellor—
August 1, 1987 — December 31, 1999

$\mathcal{W}$ hen George Sweeting was asked to serve as Moody's sixth president, he urged his predecessor, William Culbertson, to consider becoming the school's chancellor. As chancellor, he would represent the school to its fifty thousand alumni, occasionally contact some of Moody's donors, as well as speak at conferences nationally and even internationally. Precedent had been established when James Gray had become the school's first chancellor under President Will Houghton.

During the first month of Sweeting's presidency, he received a phone call from the famous news commentator Lowell Thomas requesting the opportunity of visiting Moody Bible Institute. For more than three decades, Thomas was the voice of the evening news, as well as the creator of Cinerama. As a world traveler he had frequently met Moody graduates who impressed him. Dr. Culbertson also attended the luncheon hosted by Dr. Sweeting. Recognizing Dr. Culbertson as the senior member of the group, Lowell Thomas asked Dr. Culbertson what were his responsibilities around the school. Modestly, he said that he had just been named Chancellor, to which Thomas laughed and said, "So you've been kicked upstairs!" Everyone enjoyed a good laugh.

In reality, the position of chancellor is more than a transition slot awaiting retirement. For Dr. Culbertson, however, four months later he was in the presence of the Lord. On November 16, 1971, after suffering for several months and after a reasonably peaceful day, he quoted a favorite Bible verse, "Alleluia! For the Lord God Omnipotent reigns" (Revelation 19:6). And then quietly he said, "God, God . . . yes!" and passed away.

Sweeting called the school to a major campus expansion. If the Moody Bible Institute was to remain in the city, it would need every available piece of land for growth. Also, having been a student from 1942 to 1945, with no campus but the city streets, Sweeting felt an urgency to develop an oasis-like campus. That meant tearing down the *original* 153 building as well as many other buildings. These were not easy decisions.

The city of Chicago, which had been helpful in the past, entered into an even closer relationship under Sweeting's tenure. While serving as senior pastor of the Moody Church, Sweeting had served on one of Mayor Richard J. Daley's committees during the 1968 city riots. However, George Sweeting credits Moody Vice President Marvin Beckman for his tireless efforts in building a successful relationship with the city of Chicago. Without the help of city friends, the Moody Miracle could not have happened.

The city of Chicago urged MBI to build a parking structure so that student and institutional growth could take place. The money for this was raised under the Century II program, which was launched at Founder's Week 1984.

For decades the school's library was located on the 6th and 7th floors of Crowell Hall. Along with the urgent need for library expansion was the equally pressing need for additional classroom space. Plans evolved for a Missions Academic building to be built north of Torrey-Gray auditorium on LaSalle Street. Though Dr. Sweeting shared considerably in raising the funds for this project, it would fall to Dean of Education Dr. Howard Whaley and new President Dr. Joseph Stowell to see the building erected.

It came as a total surprise when the trustees announced on dedication day, April 28, 1992, that the building would be called "The Sweeting Center for World Evangelization." Moody Board Chairman William Mitchell asked Dr. Sweeting publicly how he felt about the building being named in his honor. He answered, "I feel like I ought to be dead." Dr. Sweeting was overwhelmed yet greatly honored.

When George Sweeting agreed to serve as president in 1971, he committed himself to a fifteen-year time frame. However, in light of Moody's one-hundredth birthday in 1986, he agreed to extend his commitment to July 31, 1987.

When the trustees were convinced that Dr. Sweeting was determined to relinquish the presidency, they asked him to lead the search for his successor.

During several trustee meetings, they majored on what kind of a president was needed for the new millennium. The meetings were given to prayer, discussion, and the importance of keeping their search in confidence.

Dr. Sweeting was asked to share his thoughts about the future president of Moody Bible Institute. His comments: The president . . .

1. . . . *should have a deep love for the Moody Bible Institute.*

2. . . . *should primarily be a teacher and preacher of the Bible . . . able to express himself forcefully in speaking to large audiences.*

3. . . . *should have the gift of administration—to see that the lines of authority are clear so that the ministry continues effectively.*

4. . . . *must be committed to the Bible as the inspired, inerrant Word of God and to the doctrinal statement of the Moody Bible Institute.*

5. . . . *should be separated unto Jesus Christ and from the world, though we want to be known primarily for what we are for rather than what we are against.*

6. . . . *must be committed to the Moody Bible Institute as a single purpose college and graduate school for the purpose of training Christian workers.*

7. . . . ideally should not be an activist in areas of great controversy among evangelicals. The president should be able to work with both separatists and evangelicals.

8. Careful consideration should be given to age, health, marriage, family, education, and reputation. Regarding education, the CEO of Moody does not have to have an earned doctorate, though it would be a bonus. Though it is necessary for the Dean of Faculty and Dean of Education to have the appropriate degrees, the president must possess people skills to a high degree.

9. The president should be a visionary who is able to develop plans and programs to enhance the ministries of Moody Bible Institute—under the guidance and authority of the board of trustees.

The search committee enjoyed working together. A marvelous unity characterized the proceedings, climaxing with a unanimous decision to call Joseph M. Stowell III. Dr. Stowell began his presidency August 1, 1987.

Sweeting said, "The transition was all I could have dreamed. The ministry continued without missing a beat and Dr. Stowell has taken the school to new heights—to the glory of God."

Both Sweeting and Stowell felt an urgent need for a state of the art physical fitness center, primarily to teach future Christian leaders lifelong physical health that could enhance and extend their usefulness. The intensity of inner-city life also made a facility of this nature desirable.

In the fall of 1988, Dr. Sweeting was leading a Bible conference in the city of Phoenix, Arizona. One morning the daily paper carried a story about Karsten and Louise Solheim of Ping golf equipment fame, and a substantial gift given to a local university for a physical fitness center.

Dr. Sweeting knew the Solheim family primarily through their oldest son Louis, who had been a student in Moody's one-year advanced study program. That week Dr. Sweeting phoned the Solheims and requested an appointment. The meeting took place on October 7 at the Moon Valley Country Club. The Solheims were well acquainted with Moody through their son Lou and also through the ministry of Moody Institute of Science. The fellowship that day was choice. Following an enjoyable lunch, Dr. Sweeting congratulated the Solheims on their generous gift to the local university. He then shared Moody's need for a world-class fitness center. The idea caught fire.

That meeting resulted in a request to Dr. Sweeting to secure plans for the kind of facility Moody had in mind.

In concert with others at Moody, a Boston company—which specialized in complexes of that nature—designed a winner. Tracy Sumner, in the book *Karsten's Way*, writes,

> Once Karsten saw the plans for the beautiful basketball court, practice gyms, workout rooms, weight-training center, racquetball courts, and Olympic-sized swimming pool, he and Louise agreed to underwrite the cost. Moody Bible Institute honored this commitment by naming the facility the Solheim Center. The result is such a gem that the building is considered on a par with some of the finest in the world.
>
> Several National Basketball Association teams work out at the Solheim Center when they come to town to play the Chicago Bulls. The NBA rookie camp has been held there more than once. Even the Dream Team, the US Olympic basketball team made up of the best of the NBA, has practiced there. But, more important to the Solheims, the Institute has not kept the center exclusively for the use of its own students and NBA teams. MBI opens the building on *selected days* for the use of local, inner-city ministries, giving underprivileged children access to facilities they might not otherwise ever see, let alone play in.

The Solheim Center was completed and dedicated on January 30, 1991. Needless to say, it's a popular building in the lives of students, employees, and friends.

As chancellor of Moody Bible Institute, George Sweeting kept an energetic schedule. He has continued to serve as a trustee since 1969. For more than thirty years he has been a regular broadcaster over the

Moody Network. Each issue of *Moody* magazine has carried an article by him since 1971. In the last five years he has written five books for Moody Press. One of his greatest joys has been leading an annual trip to Israel along with his pastor son, Dr. Donald Sweeting. George Sweeting has served well to the glory of God.

Many years ago, while a student at MBI, George Sweeting was told that he might not live the year out, due to testicular cancer. Yet on June 14, 1997, Hilda and George celebrated fifty years of marriage. Some two hundred friends came to celebrate God's faithfulness.

Jokingly, Dr. Stowell occasionally reminds Dr. Sweeting that he can't wait to get his job as chancellor. Early in 1999 Dr. Sweeting felt it was time for another transition—now chancellor emeritus—as of December 31, 1999.

The announcement resulted in an outpouring of tributes like these:

> *I am delighted to join with your many, many friends in extending congratulations on your magnificent service to Moody and the Kingdom. This is a grand occasion when Moody is justly recognizing you as Chancellor Emeritus.*
>
> *I think back to the earliest days of my Christian life. You were one of the first leaders I met; at a time when so many people were so skeptical of my conversion, you welcomed me with open arms. I shall never forget the warm smile and embrace that you gave me. You became a role model for me in those days, and you have continued to be one over the years.*
>
> *I have always enjoyed our times of fellowship. I have appreciated your writing and your messages. Most of all, I have respected your statesman-like stature. You have provided strength and stability and great inspiration to the body of Christ as a whole.*
>
> *Yours in His service*
> *Charles W. Colson*
> *Prison Fellowship Ministries*

Beloved friend George,

I have known you for fifty-seven years. The late Dr. Robert G. Lee respected you, even as I respect you, although he did not know you as well as I know you. He referred to you as a young man who "measures twelve inches to the foot, thirty-six inches to the yard and strikes twelve for God." I agree.

God used you to captain the great Moody Bible Institute/College ship through treacherous shoals and stormy seas in some of the most demanding days of our history. I think of the superb leadership you gave through the seventies and eighties when extremists on all sides were weakening organizations through their precipitous actions. Never once did you project a doctrinaire position. Oh yes, you projected a fidelity to the doctrine — to the "faith once and for all delivered to the saints." But you were not an ideologue. You were God's Faithful servant.

> *Affectionately and prayerfully,*
> *John Edmund Haggai, Founder & Chairman*
> *Haggai Institute*

Dear Doc,

Congratulations on your wonderful ministry at Moody, and the lives you have touched for Christ. I count myself blessed to be one who has learned from you, been loved by you, and had the joy of great times with you. I thank the Lord on every reminder of you and the major impact you have on my life. Hardly a day passes without my thinking, "what would Doc do?" Wish I did what you would more often than I do!

> *Your friend in Christ,*
> *Jim Gwinn, President*
> *Crista Ministries*

Dear Dr. Sweeting,

Almost thirty years have passed since we first met. I was a young pastor at Edgewater Baptist Church, and you encouraged me in the ministry. When I joined the faculty at Moody Bible Institute, you gave me the privilege of speaking at pastors' conferences and the like. Somehow I felt as if I were your son; later, I discovered that many young men felt the same kind of acceptance and encouragement.

When I agonized whether to accept the call to become pastor of Moody Church, you again encouraged me (my youth not withstanding). I can still recall your fervent prayer given at my installation twenty years ago.

> *Thanks for a life well lived.*
> *Erwin W. Lutzer, Senior Pastor*
> *The Moody Church*

Dear Dr. Sweeting,

It was a September day in 1968 when Mary and I met you at Moody Church. Little did we realize that meeting would result in such a close and long lasting affiliation and friendship.

Your years of service to the Lord and MBI are of inestimable value. The work has been greatly enhanced as God has used your innovative ability and warm heart for people. Thanks for that ministry to all of us, and especially, to MJ and me.

> *Warmly in His name,*
> *E. Brandt Gustavson, President*
> *National Religious Broadcasters*

Dear George,

We praise God for these many years that you and Hilda have served the Lord there at Moody Bible Institute. During your years as president and then chancellor, the Lord has continued to bless and use the Institute, and thousands of students have been equipped for life, and for the Lord's service around the world.

Now as you become Chancellor Emeritus and try to cut back your schedule a little bit, we pray for God's continued richest blessing on you and Hilda. We thank God for your faithfulness and commitment down through these many years, and praise Him for the many gifts He entrusted to you not only in administration, but through your writing, speaking, and radio ministry.

As MBI honors you, Ruth and I want to join your many friends in sending our warmest congratulations.

> *Cordially yours,*
> *Dr. Billy Graham*

Dear Dad,

You've always had an innate sense of timing. I saw it when you stepped down as president, and again when you decided that your time as chancellor was up.

The Lord has been so good to you and to our whole family. Moody Bible Institute has been a special part of that blessing.

Thank you MBI for being a channel of God's goodness to my mom and dad. Thank you Lord for your abundant and sustaining grace over the years. And thank you Dad for serving so well. WE are so proud of you today. You have served faithfully and finished well. You have given people like me another example of how to do it right.

And thank you Mom, for standing alongside Dad in this ministry. Your lifelong role as wife, mom, and grandmother enabled him to do the work he did. While Dad has received most of the public credit, we all know that this has been a ministry partnership all through the years, and you have been its secret strength.

> *Don Sweeting, Senior Pastor*
> *Cherry Creek Presbyterian Church*

19

The Sweeting Legacy

From the beginning, the Moody Bible Institute has been a team effort. In the late 1800s the team consisted of Emma Dryer, D. L. Moody, Reuben A. Torrey, and a host of others. To be sure, Moody was the human instrument that provided the team's greatness, yet without the others, the dream would have died.

George Sweeting is a unique part of Moody's history in that he is the only graduate to serve both as senior pastor of the church Moody founded and as president and chancellor of the Moody Bible Institute. He has also served as a trustee longer than any other president.

Sweeting's parents spoke often of D. L. Moody's impact upon Scotland and indirectly upon their own lives. However, it was as a student of the Moody Bible Institute from 1942 to 1945 that George Sweeting studied Moody's life and work seriously.

Sweeting's love of history in general and D. L. Moody in particular enabled him to focus on Moody's passion. He regularly reminded students and employees alike that world evangelization was Moody's heartbeat. With great enthusiasm he would tell how John R. Mott, Robert Wilder, and D. L. Moody coined the motto in 1886, "Our supreme task is world evangelization in this generation." The Sweeting legacy includes a recommitment to D. L. Moody's all-consuming passion.

Early in his presidency, Sweeting reestablished the school's allegiance to the city of Chicago and the urban centers of the world.

The 1960s and 1970s witnessed an evangelical exodus from the cities to the suburbs nationwide. As many inner-city schools moved, Moody Bible Institute was also tempted. Several trustees privately and publicly urged Sweeting to relocate to the wide-open spaces. One trustee located a Catholic campus that was for sale in the western suburbs and arranged for the trustees to visit it. Another friend of the Institute located a one-thousand acre tract of land in southern Wisconsin and offered to help acquire the land on the condition that Moody Bible Institute would relocate.

Sweeting listened carefully and then proceeded to convince the donor that Moody Bible Institute was located where it could best model Christ's love for the cities of the world. Sweeting then guided the trustees to a unanimous recommitment to their historic location.

Out of this recommitment to Chicago, a plan evolved to acquire adjacent land for development. This thrust has continued unabated for more than thirty years and is part of the Sweeting/Stowell legacy. Although many people have contributed to campus expansion, no one has done more than former Senior Vice President Marvin Beckman, affectionately nicknamed "the acre taker."

In the early 1970s, homes and factories lined Wells Street from Chicago Avenue to Division Street. Acquiring such properties was considered nearly impossible. New challenges were presented in every trustee meeting. Millions of dollars were spent to purchase, demolish, and rebuild . . . until today more than five city streets and twenty-three acres are part of the Moody campus. This miracle, supported and encouraged by generous trustees, is part of the Sweeting/Stowell legacy.

Early in the Sweeting presidency, a three-year evangelistic mailing program was launched to reach every family in the city of Chicago. A choice letter was sent from Dr. Sweeting, which shared the gospel in an appealing way, along with a booklet similar to the Four Spiritual

Laws and an offer of a free correspondence course. Thousands responded. During the first year, the mailings went to the southside, next year to the westside, and the third year to the northside. More than two million pieces of mail were sent to the people of Chicago.

Many indicated they wanted to make a profession of faith. Student and employee teams visited and discipled hundreds of Chicagoans. Evangelism has always been a vital part of the Moody Bible Institute, and this expenditure of effort and dollars underscored Moody's historic commitment.

Along with others, George Sweeting saw the importance of expanding Moody radio. Early in 1975 a Chicago businessman offered to underwrite a weekly television broadcast featuring Dr. Sweeting. The businessman would pay all bills until the telecast was self-sustaining. This was an extraordinary offer; however, after much prayer and discussion, it was concluded that Moody's expertise was radio rather than television. The decision resulted in a plan to expand Moody Broadcasting from three owned and operated stations to as many as possible. That also led to the founding of the Moody Radio Network in 1982. Today the Moody Bible Institute owns and operates thirty commercial-free stations and supplies radio programs for 680 affiliates via satellite.

Runaway inflation characterized the 1970s. Mortgage rates jumped to 16 percent and homes tripled in value in the space of several years. Salaries also increased more than 60 percent. Moody soon faced a serious financial problem. After much prayer and care, the Sweeting administration pursued several approaches.

It decided to tell supporters about opportunities and needs in a more personal way. A monthly letter was sent to friends in place of a printed quarterly report. Mailing lists were reviewed and pruned. Lists were segmented and tested, resulting in an immediate response. Gently yet definitely Moody told its financial needs, and friends began to respond.

Since the days of Henry Parson Crowell, Moody has been blessed with a choice stewardship department. However, this area needed an infusion of personnel and ideas. Resource Development, Inc. was hired to retrain staff. Goals were carefully established and reached. The approach was "full information and gentle solicitation." The efforts were blessed so that even today the Institute receives wills and bequests written in those challenging days.

The Sweeting legacy also includes increasing the student body and expanding Moody's educational program to a four-year undergraduate and graduate level. In 1972 an advanced studies program was launched for college graduates who needed a Bible study emphasis. In time this evolved into Moody's graduate school.

During the late 1970s, several graduates from the three-year diploma program were refused visas to carry out missionary service. Some nations determined that entering missionaries needed to have at least a four-year college degree. After operating without a degree program for more than ninety years, several trustees were hesitant to change. However, a year's study resulted in unanimous approval to grant degrees. Much credit for these programs must be shared with Moody's gifted faculty, especially former deans Howard Whaley, Robert Woodburn, and Wayne Hopkins. The program continues to grow and expand under the leadership of President Stowell.

At heart, George Sweeting will always be a pastor and an evangelist. Early in his tenure he felt the need to encourage and edify pastors and Christian workers. On a trial basis he launched a pastors' conference in 1972, designed to inspire and support. This initiative met with immediate success. To this day, each May pastors arrive from most of the states and Canada for encouragement, instruction, and networking. Pastors report that after spending a week in Moody's classrooms, dormitories, and dining room, they feel like alumni. The annual Pastors' Conference is an important part of the Sweeting legacy.

Recently a writer for the student newspaper asked Dr. Sweeting what his legacy was to the Moody Bible Institute. He answered, "I don't really think much about that, but I do think about being faithful to Jesus Christ."

President Stowell in an interview with Kristin Barnhill for the student paper said, "The greatest part of the Sweeting legacy is marked in his character. He's always been a man of great character and integrity. You always trusted Dr. Sweeting. Even after years of service, his stellar character provided an example to students and created a broad platform of respect. When a leader does this, the whole institution rises to that level."

Probably George Sweeting's greatest legacy is his example of a godly life. Often he prefaces or concludes his remarks with the words of Psalm 115:1, "Not unto us, O Lord, not unto us. But to Your name give glory."

20

Unforgettable Quotations from George Sweeting

1. Seldom repress a generous impulse.

2. Watch your beginnings! It is important to begin well and supremely important to end well.

3. A Christian is the combination of Christ and you.

4. Every problem in life is a chance to display God's power.

5. Salvation is an offer, not a demand.

6. Ordinary ability when focused excels!

7. Discipline plus determination determines destiny.

8. God is the perfect steward!

9. Prayer and work are a powerful New Testament combination.

10. Constant assurance of salvation depends upon practical obedience to the Word of God.

11. Success is found in allowing the Holy Spirit undisputed control.

12. We are what we are because of what we do with our God-given opportunities.

13. The main thing in life is to keep the main thing the main thing.

14. *Excuses only satisfy the people who make them.*

15. *Excellence is more than a wish; it's a lifetime pursuit.*

16. *The desire to excel is neither crass nor carnal but rather an inborn yearning to mimic God.*

17. *Life minus God's love equals zero.*

18. *Jesus never gained disciples falsely. He never hid His scars but plainly said, "Behold My hands and My feet."*

19. *The person fully surrendered to Jesus has solved the problem of worldliness.*

20. *The Dead Sea is the Dead Sea because it always receives and never gives.*

21. *People with burdens need the church just like sick people need a hospital.*

22. *When I come to the close of life, the question will be "How much have I given?" not "How much have I gotten?"*

23. *The cross is a giant sign of addition announcing the generous nature of God.*

24. *The secret of the victorious Christian life is found in a series of new beginnings.*

21

Personal Essays by George Sweeting

MY BOYHOOD PASTOR

Since it began in 1925, the Hawthorne Gospel Church has hosted guests such as Harry Ironside, Donald Grey Barnhouse, Martin Lloyd Jones, Robert G. Lee, A. W. Tozer, and Billy Graham. For the first sixty-two years, the church had the same pastor, a man who never became well known. When asked why he stayed so long at the same place, Herrmann George Braunlin modestly answered, "No one ever asked me to leave."

My boyhood pastor was a role model for me and many others. During a lifetime of ministry, I have regularly asked myself, "How would Pastor Braunlin handle this situation?"

Even though he never attended college or seminary, he was a capable teacher, talented administrator, and brilliant visionary. Seldom have I seen a more innovative church than Hawthorne Gospel Church. Forty years ago Pastor Braunlin advised the congregation to relocate to choice acreage along a strategic highway leading directly to New York City. Few agreed with his vision for relocation at first, yet today all enthusiastically agree that it was a move of genius.

Other of his programs included "Bible House," which retailed

Christian literature to a major metropolitan area; a quality evening school that has greatly influenced the area for more than fifty years; a lending library used by churches of every denomination; a day-care center; and a secondary school—all in addition to conventional church outreaches. During his lifetime he received significant honors. But he was a genuinely humble man who did not mention his awards to his congregation.

Pastor Braunlin was a man of the Bible and of prayer. He faithfully taught the Bible, verse by verse, from Genesis 1:1 to Revelation 22:21. And regardless the occasion, earnest prayer was the norm. To him, praying was as necessary as breathing.

Each of us needs at least three people in our life: a Paul, a Barnabas, and a Timothy. A Barnabas is an equal partner in ministry, and a Timothy is a younger person in the faith who is eager to learn and grow. But Pastor Braunlin was a Paul to me—a beloved friend and counselor.

On October 5, 1995, Herrmann G. Braunlin was promoted into the presence of God. More than one thousand friends attended his memorial service to express affection for him and to give thanks to God for a loving, hardworking pastor.

Thankfully, each of us has an Eternal Pastor who is always available and has promised to *never* leave us (Hebrews 13:5). He remains the author and *finisher* of our faith.

MY ANGEL MOTHER

"Kilmore College" was the name of my mother's childhood home in Carstairs Junction, Scotland. Her mother, Annie McKerrow Irving, died while giving birth to her third child, leaving her husband, George Irving, to care for my mother, her brother Isaac, and the newborn, Annie.

Life was hard in the Irving home, filled with sadness. Her father found it impossible to work and handle his three young children as a single parent. At first, he hired a housekeeper who moved in with the children. Eventually he married a widow with children and added them to the Irving household. Living conditions became so stressful that my mother's brother, Isaac, left home at age fourteen and joined the Navy, while their sister, Annie, ran away, never to be heard from again. The George Irving family occasionally attended the village congregational church. Several of the family are buried in the cemetery there.

Though my mother's childhood had its share of sorrows, she experienced a marvelous transformation in her teenage years. An acquaintance named Jesse Kay, whom I met decades later, began a girls' club in Carstairs Junction. After several visits, my mother, Mary Rodger Irving, was converted to Christ. She was bright, winsome, and committed to spiritual growth. Her new faith made her home situation at least tolerable.

My father, William Sweeting, after returning from fighting in Belgium in World War I with the Royal British Engineers, picked up his trade as a stonemason. His work brought him into the village of Carstairs Junction, where he worked on the building of a large stone bridge over the town's railroad station. It was there my parents met. My mother quickly shared her faith, telling of her life's transformation. She also urged my father to visit two centers in Glasgow, Scotland—Bethany Hall and Tent Hall—where he could hear more about the new life she had discovered.

Because of my father's war experience and the chaos of life in general, he was anxious to visit Bethany Hall and was marvelously converted. The change in his life was so evident that his father feared William was a fanatic. His conversion led to eventual courtship and marriage in 1920 to Mary Rodger Irving, who would become my mother.

Tired of the wars of Europe and eager for the opportunity to better themselves, they immigrated to the United States in 1923.

Though my father was the unquestioned head of the home, my mother was the heart of the home. Along with a deep faith, she possessed a loving, cheerful disposition. She gave birth to six children: William James, Anne McKerrow, George, Norman, Mary Beattie, and Martha Jean.

Late in the 1940s she was afflicted with rheumatoid and osteo-arthritis. At times her affliction was so intense that she was bedfast. Her hands became deformed and her joints gnarled. Yet even in suffering she was an overcomer. With the advent of cortisone, she managed with great difficulty to get about the home. Her faith was obvious to all who came to visit. Amid constant pain and discomfort, she displayed a triumphant spirit and a gentle sense of humor.

Her three sons entered the ministry and served an aggregate of 150 years. In my mother's eyes, serving God and people is the highest calling possible. From time to time, my mother eloquently exhorted her preacher sons, and we would teasingly call her "the best preacher in the Sweeting family." All through her life, till her homegoing, she was to us a ministering angel.

REMEMBERING THE FATHER

Call him Dad, Pop, Papa . . . everyone has a father. My father was very special to me while I was growing up. He was a provider, protector, and priest for our family.

As provider, he did whatever was necessary to maintain a roof over our heads, clothing on our backs, and enough food to eat. As protector, he held the family together, carefully guiding and guarding the children. But above and beyond everything else, my father was the priest and spiritual leader of our family. On occasion, when it was necessary to discipline us, he would say, "As spiritual head of the home, and in view of a future day when I will give account of my family to God, I am responsible to discipline you." Needless to say, his approach gained our attention, respect, and gratitude.

My memories of my father are wholesome. He was hardworking, well organized, and very serious. He never took a seminar in fatherhood, nor did he ever read a book about parenting, but by virtue of marriage he fathered six children, and that meant guiding and leading his family.

Though my parents often read to us about God's love, they did not specifically teach us about it but rather modeled divine love in their everyday family living.

My dad was, without doubt, the head of our home, and no one ever wanted it any other way. At times he even lost his temper, especially when we got the giggles while he read the Bible at the evening meal. Being immigrant children, we, on rare occasions, laughed at his Scottish pronunciation of certain words. His brogue could be comical.

He was punctual to a fault so that, to this day, I abhor tardiness. His life was well ordered and we were sensitive to his routine. I can still see him sitting in the same chair each night after supper, reading his "untouched newspaper." None of the six children would think of opening it until he had finished reading it.

Though he worked hard all his life, rarely taking a vacation, he never accumulated much money. Wistfully he would comment that God couldn't trust him with riches. He was upset by waste of any form. Only one light was allowed to shine in any given room.

He loathed deceit. His life was built on principles he refused to violate. His word was as binding and sacred as a signed legal contract.

Though the memories of my brothers and sisters vary, we all agree as to his pure faith in Christ. His commitment to pass on the faith to his children was so great that he changed churches to make sure his children were exposed to a dynamic practical application of the Scriptures.

My father taught us many things. He helped us grow up secure, healthy, and open to the will of God. He challenged us to be and give our best. He taught us submission to him and to the government, but first and foremost to God.

He taught us truthfulness and the folly of dishonesty. He urged us never to fear standing alone, as long as we were compassionate with others. He taught us that the call of God was the highest call in the world, and the glory of God was our chief motivation. He taught us that we are to be God's faithful stewards.

I'm eternally grateful to God for a father like that.

MY VERY BEST FRIEND

I met my life's partner on a toboggan slope . . . resulting in a fifty-year run. I had watched her at a distance at local church functions and liked what I saw. Margaret Hilda Schnell was shy, pretty, friendly, and spiritual. Our first dates consisted of church activities, services in hospitals, jails, and rescue missions. Both of us were caught up in the excitement of an area-wide series of meetings at the First Baptist Church of Paterson, New Jersey. The meeting lasted for forty-one days—and we never missed a service. George T. Stevens was the evangelist greatly used to bring a spiritual awakening to our area.

During that series we both began seriously to share our faith with others and consider the possibility of future Christian service. Those meetings also gave us a needed excuse to see each other and the chance for an occasional soda at the Paradise Restaurant. Because money was scarce in the Sweeting family, Hilda often bailed me out.

Our only means of travel was public transportation, which meant that I traveled from the town of Haledon and she from the town of Fairlawn. Hilda's parents had immigrated from Seigen, Germany, in 1923, and my parents had come from Glasgow, Scotland, that same year. Our fathers had fought against each other in Belgium in World War I. Both fathers, after their conversions, decided to leave Europe for America.

As teenagers, I worked delivering milk while Hilda worked in her father's bakery at 14-12 River Road. Often I would leave a quart of chocolate milk at her back door and find, in exchange, a bag of the best tasting goodies ever made. I got the best of the deal.

We prayed earnestly about our friendship. Under the heading of ambitions, my high school yearbook says "to be an evangelist and artist." Because we sensed God's call we enrolled and graduated from Moody Bible Institute. Our time there was incredible. We were challenged to be our best and to give our best. Weekends found us serving in rallies and churches throughout the Midwest.

In those days I would illustrate my messages by drawing a large, dramatic scene in chalk on a six-foot-wide canvas board. Background music helped the audience focus on the scene as multicolored lights produced dazzling effects. The finished drawing became an illustration for the sermon that followed. Both of us enjoyed the work and realized how we were being prepared to serve together.

On June 14, 1947, wedding bells announced our marriage. Over the years our love has grown. In looking back, I could not have found a more fitting partner. Her steadfast love of our children and me has been a source of enormous stability and strength.

We view our partnership as a special gift from God. We do not pretend even for a moment that we were bright enough to make the right choices. However, with great gratitude and utter humility, we give thanks.

WILLIAM JAMES SWEETING: 1511 A.D.

William James Sweeting was the name reserved for our firstborn son, according to our Scottish tradition. The name can be traced back for many generations in our family. That was my father's name as well as my older brother's.

The name "Sweeting" is English, though for generations the Sweetings lived in Scotland. On Mother's side we were part of the Irving Clan, and on my paternal grandmother's side, the MacDonald Clan. The name "Sweeting" is listed in the unabridged dictionary. It is a noun defined as "1) a variety of sweet apple, 2) an archaic version of sweetheart."

The Christian faith can be found in our family rather consistently, though there were lean years when the witness was dim.

Recently my son Donald William Sweeting was studying *Foxe's Book of Martyrs*, a record of those who heroically stood and even gave their lives for the Christian faith. Classic illustrations are given, like that of Polycarp, Bishop of Smyrna (Asia Minor), in 69–155 A.D. Polycarp reportedly knew the apostle John as well as other disciples of Jesus. He served as a vital link between the apostolic fathers and his day.

Intense persecution broke out in Asia Minor toward the end of his life. Eleven Christians had been put to death from the area of Philadelphia (one hundred miles away). In an insane fury, the people called for the burning of Polycarp. The proconsul entreated the aged leader to recant his faith and escape the hostile crowd. To this he replied, "Eighty and six years have I served Him, and He never once wronged me; how then shall I blaspheme my King, who hath saved me?" After those final words he was tied to the stake, amid wood and straw, and burned to death. Polycarp did not doubt in the dark what God revealed in the light.

Amid the records of Foxe's unabridged edition, I found this paragraph:

> "William James Sweeting (1511) was burned to death in Smithfield, England for his commitment to the Word of God."

He was part of our family history.

I too choose to humbly follow in the steps of all those who did not doubt in the dark what God revealed in the light.

22

Select Sermons by George Sweeting

HOLDING THE ROPES

"Yonder is a gold mine, I will descend and dig, but you must hold the ropes."
William Carey, missionary to India

"Hold on. Hold on tight. Easy now! OK, he's hit ground." So the friends of Saul must have whispered, as they stealthily slipped him through a window on the Damascus wall to escape the Jews who tried to kill him.

How did Saul get into this predicament? What brought about this ill feeling against him? Just a short time before, he had been brilliant in their eyes, extremely religious and ruthless in his attempt to rid the world of the followers of Jesus. Saul had been convinced that Jesus was an impostor and that His followers were heretics. Because Saul felt that he was chosen to dispose of this threat to the Jewish belief in the unity of God, he zealously worked to capture and jail or even kill any Christians he could find.

But God Himself captured Saul. He caught him as Saul was going to Damascus to hunt Christians, and Saul went to Damascus a changed man. In fact, "He preached Jesus in the synagogues, that he is the Son of God" (Acts 9:20). The people were amazed; some were skeptical; some were furious with Saul as Saul had been with them.

Consequently Saul began to receive the treatment he had been giving out. He became a hunted man. He could no longer safely walk the streets of Damascus, for soldiers were everywhere. What was he to do? Fortunately Saul had friends, believers in Christ, who cared for him. They led him stealthily through the shadows of the city to the Damascus wall. Then, hidden in a large basket, Saul was lowered through a window (Acts 9:25; 2 Corinthians 11:33). The disciples slowly played out the ropes that held the basket until they heard it thud to the ground, and heard Saul crawl quietly out and move away into the darkness. Then they pulled up the basket and went about their business.

WHO WERE THE ROPE-HOLDERS?

We know what happened to Saul after his escape from Damascus, but what became of the disciples who held the ropes? Who were they? Where did they go? What did they do? Why were they willing to risk their lives for someone they may have just barely known?

Who were the rope-holders? Nobody knows. Nothing more is said about them. Their names are never mentioned. They remain unknown to history, unknown to us. But God knows them. And that is enough. Those disciples were truly servants, for they served without recognition.

Too often people will serve as long as they get publicity. They will donate food or clothing to poor starving people—if their names are printed in the church bulletin. They will give money to build buildings—if a plaque on the wall will carry their names.

Jesus said, "Take heed that you do not do your charitable deeds before men, to be seen by them. Otherwise you have no reward from your Father in heaven" (Matthew 6:1). In fact, He suggested such secrecy that the left hand would not know what the right hand did.

Whether or not the rope-holders knew this injunction, they weren't concerned. They did the job that was required of them, then disappeared. How many Christians do you know who serve in this way? There must be scores of doctors, mechanics, lawyers, janitors, salesclerks, teachers, secretaries, garbage collectors, executives, and homemakers who go about their business from day to day, serving Christ in their own way, doing what is required of them.

They hold the ropes, perhaps performing services that don't seem particularly Christian—on the surface, anyway. For example, do you know a mechanic who never overcharges and always has your car ready when it's promised? Or a busy mother who takes care of her neighbor's children once a week so their mother can have a few hours of quiet? These are not Christian acts performed for the public. They are part of a Christian way of life. These people follow in a tradition of rope-holders who steadfastly serve without publicity.

Perhaps the greatest rope-holders are parents. Jochebed, the mother of Moses, defied the laws of Egypt so that her baby boy would live (Exodus 2:1–9). "When she could hide him no longer, she placed Moses in a basket" and laid it in the reeds by the river's bank (v. 3). Jochebed held the ropes for her boy.

Many of us are followers of Christ because of our parents. They patiently suffered through our growing up. They loved us in spite of ourselves and continued to love us until we were ready to be on our own—until our basket touched ground. My mother and father certainly did. They prayed for me, wept over me, scolded me, and loved me. I'm sure their faithfulness kept me from wandering too far off the track. I thank God for parents who hold the ropes for their children and expect no reward. They are like those disciples who held the ropes for Saul. They hang on no matter what the circumstances.

WHEN DID THEY HOLD THE ROPES?

"The disciples took him by night and let him down by the wall in a basket."
Acts 9:25

The ropes were held by night. The escape had to be made at night, since daylight was as dangerous for the disciples as it was for Saul. But they weren't really safe at night either.

The Bible also warns us that we struggle "against the rulers of the darkness of this age, against spiritual hosts of wickedness in the heavenly places" (Ephesians 6:12).

It seems to me that it is easy to be a Christian in the daylight, when we can see where we are going and when life is uncomplicated. But what happens when darkness falls? What do we do when we are not sure what direction to take because the paths are confused? How do we react when life seems to have no point? Is that the time to forget Christ?

Some do. Peter did—for a time, at least. He was right there holding the ropes when Jesus was popular. But when trouble came, Peter denied his Lord. And Peter had been convinced that he would never do such a thing. We probably all feel like Peter at times.

Though most of us have not been in such a critical position, some Christians around the world are in constant danger. I know a pastor in East Germany who met with a group of young American Christians in the 1960s. The visiting teenagers were dumbfounded when he carefully shut all the windows even though the day was stifling. He explained that he was afraid of being overheard in a discussion of Christianity. Though this pastor could have escaped East Germany, he chose to stay with his underground church. He is holding the ropes for his flock, who worship Christ in fear for their lives. In some countries the situation is not so different from Saul's.

This is an age of opportunity, an age of excitement, but at the same time an age of terror. We have sent men into space. We have discovered ways of prolonging life. Yet we still do not understand our own world, and we still manufacture implements of war. We produce food that rots in stockpiles while millions of the world's population slowly starve to death. We send missionaries to Africa and India and South America, but our own neighbors in the ghettoes and suburbs do not hear words of love from us. It is a dark age masquerading as a world of enlightenment. Where will it end? What can you do? Hold the ropes, my friends. Hang on tight. Don't let go. God has chosen you; the missionaries you pray for count on you; your children count on you; your neighbors count on you; your church needs you. Keep holding the ropes in spite of the confusion surrounding us.

Saul's friends did not give up. Don't you.

The disciples held on until the basket touched the ground. They didn't drop it halfway because it got heavy or they got tired. Saul trusted them to hang on until he was on the ground.

Someone has said that the greatest ability is dependability. It didn't take any great ability for the disciples to hold the ropes. They just had to hang on until they were sure Saul was safe.

That's the key. Once you put yourself in a position of becoming a rope-holder, you can't give up. You can't be responsible for everybody, that's true. You'd be exhausted. But you are responsible for certain people.

For some, you may be the only one holding the ropes. What about the widow who lives next door to you? Her children all live out of town; she hasn't many friends. Who is there to care about her? Perhaps you're the only one.

Then there are those high school boys who hang around with your son. Where are their parents? Why are the kids always at your house? Maybe they need an adult friend to care about them.

And how about those men you have lunch with every day, those busy executives? Do they know anybody else who can show them Christ's love, or is it up to you?

No, you can't hold the ropes for everybody. But there are some who are your special province.

Of course, trying to be a rope-holder may be discouraging. You may serve the widow countless dinners and numerous cups of coffee and still have little chance to talk to her about Christ. Just when you think the kids really accept you, they may back away. And your business acquaintances may never want to consider what Christ has to say to them. All your praying, all your active showing of love may seem useless.

But are you looking for a reward? Or are you trying to serve Christ? Perhaps you won't see results as you serve. Then again, you might. You never know what God is going to do. You never know when your prayer will be answered or how it will be answered.

WHY DID THEY HOLD THE ROPES?

Perhaps the disciples' reason was simple: someone was in trouble and they could help. Those men didn't really know whom they were helping to escape. Oh, they knew something about Saul. They knew what he had been and what he had become. But that was all. They knew nothing of his future ministry.

They had no idea he would preach in some of the most important places in their world—Jerusalem, Antioch, and Cyprus. They didn't imagine that he would start churches all over Asia, including Corinth and Rome. They didn't dream he would write letters that would become part of the Scripture. To them he was Saul, a believer, their friend. They were not concerned with who he might be or what he might become. They were concerned about doing their job *faithfully*.

You may not know who's in your basket. When she hid him in a basket, did Moses' mother know her son would deliver his people from slavery? Did D. L. Moody's mother know what he would become? Did the people who helped Jews escape Germany during World War II know what their charges would become? Do you suppose Lee Harvey Oswald's or Sirhan Sirhan's role in history might have been different if someone had been holding the ropes for them?

None of us really knows about the people we carry in our baskets. But we all have someone. And we must be faithful—as Christ is faithful to us. God doesn't give us a bigger task than we can handle. But He expects us to do the job assigned to us. David did his job with a sling. Gideon did his with a vase. An unknown woman did hers with a vial of oil. Rahab, the harlot, held the ropes for two Jewish spies (Joshua 2:9) and as a result, she's included in Hebrews 11:31. She also became a part of the genealogy of Jesus (Matthew 1:5) because of her rope-holding faith.

Are we holding the ropes for the people God has given us? Will we hang on until their baskets safely touch ground?

God has called us to be servants. He has called us to be rope-holders in a dying world.

HOW TO REACH OUR CITIES

The city is here to stay. We must not ignore, deplore, or flee it forever. At the present time 90 percent of the earth's inhabitants live in 5 percent of the earth's area. Within the next century it is claimed that thirty billion people may live in a universal city that covers the globe. Already the United States is a metropolitan society, with at least 60 percent of its population clustered in the cities. Within the urban areas the masses of coming generations will work out their destinies. In the cities the future of America will be decided for better or for worse.

While the population of the cities mounts and continues, many Christians are selling out and moving to the suburbs. For example, one evangelical denomination once had five churches within the city limits of a major city. It now has but one. An evangelical withdrawal has been taking place for many years. In fact, we have been running down a road of retreat in other areas. We have seen this as part of a general retreat from the world. We pulled out first to build our own Bible schools, seminaries, and colleges. The body of Christ has farther and farther estranged itself from our society by developing "separate but equal" facilities in such things as insurance, cruises, entertainment, retirement communities, book clubs, record clubs, and so on. Now, in effect, we are building our own cities.

Christians often equate their faith with nice people, blue skies, smiles, and upper-class goals. In rural America the Protestant is dominant; in fact, the *conservative* Protestant is dominant. His attitudes and style of life set the tone for the whole society—the respectable standard—the American way. But in the city the Protestant is a distinct minority. Jews and Jewish values are influential. Roman Catholics far outnumber Protestants, operate far bigger church programs. By the time you add a sprinkling of multiple small sects from a melting pot of cultures, you come up with one sure thing: in the city the Protestant lifestyle is not dominant.

This means that the evangelical who encounters the city does so with considerable culture shock. The conservative Protestant feels uneasy about being a minority. Culture shock gives the feeling of being trapped in a situation you do not fully understand. One writer explains it like this: "A tourist travels through a strange culture protected by the cocoon of his own culture which he takes along with him. All the strange ways strike him as being quaint. He knows he will leave them soon for the security of his well-known and well-loved ways. These quaint attitudes and manners of the foreign then become the topic of conversation and much laughter with the old friends back home. But when he moves into a foreign culture there is no escape back into the familiar. The quaint ways soon lose their quaintness and are despised. There is increasing nostalgia for the old that remembers only the best . . . the quaint are now paying the piper, and if he wants to dance he must do so in their tune."

The majority of evangelicals have long held an anticity attitude, associating the city with Sodom and Gomorrah, scarlet women, crime, and filth. This antiurban bias has kept us from penetrating three great segments of the world's population: Hindus, Muslims, and modern city dwellers. Somehow we must come to realize this attitude is suicidal to the church of Jesus Christ.

A few months ago I was visiting in one of the smaller cities of the Midwest. A couple greeted me and took me in hand almost immediately. They soon were extending their condolences to me for ministering in the city of Chicago (wicked, wild, and windy). "Dr. Sweeting," they said, "the only sensible solution is to move out." I shuddered inwardly, and then patiently and (I hope) lovingly told them of God's compassion for our cities.

It seems inconceivable that at this point in the world's history, thousands of Christians still think like this.

WHY MINISTER IN THE URBAN CENTERS?

Why should we minister in the city centers? The churches of the New Testament set the example.

The apostles concentrated their efforts in the throbbing cities of their day. The ministries in those metropolitan areas were life-and-death struggles. The environment was not easy or compatible with the revolutionary new values introduced by the disciples of Christ.

Ephesus, located at the mouth of the Cayster River, was notorious for its luxury and moral looseness. Diana was the chief object of worship, and opposition to the gospel was fierce.

Corinth, with a population of six hundred thousand, was the largest city in Greece. It was an important seaport, a garrison town, and a strategic highway junction. The Corinthians were particularly prone to sexual promiscuity and enjoyed dragging each other off to court over any little difference of opinion. The city seethed with a mass of merchants, philosophers, ex-soldiers, and peddlers of vice.

Rome, metropolitan center of the Roman Empire, was riddled with perversions, court plots, and murders. Its prosperity and immorality eventually brought about its downfall.

In these centers of life, Christianity took root and flowered throughout the known world. The disciples went neither to the fringes of the towns nor to the tents of the migrants. They saw no future for the gospel in isolation. They moved into the heart of the cities—into the synagogues, the marketplaces, and the busy streets.

Today the city and its ways are increasingly setting the pace of our national life. The city has invaded our homes through the mass media and has attracted our youth. Rather than bewail the evil influence of the city and yearn for a Christian rural past that will not return, we rather ought to face with zest the adventure of learning to live Christianity in a city-dominated culture. God did not give His Son because He loved the little cluster of people in the church but because He loved the world, the adventure-seeking, reckless world—where the action is.

John Goodwin, formerly with InterVarsity, writes, "Much of our drive to build separate but equal facilities (for use by evangelicals) is the desire to forget the war we are in. We can't forget it very well with drunks stumbling over our feet, so we go to 'Christian' hotels. Non-Christians upset us, not so much because they curse and carouse (we have worse sins of our own), but because they remind us of evaded responsibility. From time to time this guilt gets intolerable (down deep we do love Christ), so we mount our chrome-trimmed chargers, and like knights of old, we gallop out of our castles in search of the dragon. We usually find him in jail, or a skid-row mission or other captive audience (even a fraternity) where we can dump our gospel load and get out again with a minimum of personal involvement of time wasted. Then back to the castle we tear, mission completed. With the drawbridge slammed shut behind us, we sing 'Safe Am I' and settle down again. Often our castle is psychological, but none the less real."

Jesus prayed, "I pray not that thou shouldest take them out of the world"; yet what Christ did not want the Father to do, we ourselves are doing when we withdraw. We try to create a monastic existence in order to avoid temptations and to live a more "godly" life, but this is a foolish underestimation of the devil's wiles and a perversion of the Great Commission.

WHAT ATTITUDES SHOULD WE HAVE?

We need to look at our attitudes concerning both God and the city.

An Attitude of Faith in God. If we are to reach our urban age, we need to cultivate an attitude of holy optimism. I am an optimist because of the sovereignty of God. Paul expresses this attitude in several places; for instance, "If God be for us, who can be against us?" (Romans 8:31). And again he exclaims, "Thanks be to God, which giveth us the victory through our Lord Jesus Christ" (1 Corinthians 15:57). Alone we can only be dragged into the mire of the city. The city exposes and bruises and tears us. But much of what the urban culture uncovers in us is sick and needs to be laid before the healing powers of Jesus Christ.

The apostolic church faced mountainous problems with complete confidence in God. "God is able" was their password into pagan territory. Only a fool would have attempted in human strength what they did. Ancient Israel met defeat at Kadesh-Barnea because the people doubted God's ability to see them through. They forgot too soon. The miracle of the Red Sea, the provision of the manna, all faded from their minds, as they considered their own weakness. Problems? Yes, they had problems. We have problems. Each of us faces his own little custom-designed set of temptations and problems. And as we enter the city world, we have individual areas of vulnerability that need to be exposed continually to the help that comes only from the Lord. Every one of us—at our point of great weakness—has a magnificent chance to display God's power. "If God be for us, who can be against us?"

True, the more we insert ourselves into the world, the more we encounter the agents from the headquarters of evil. If we are to go to the world, we cannot hide our eyes and hope the enemy will go away. Here we have to face him and take him on. But we have access to a power greater than Satan. We have Christ in us. He is our hope. When we step out into the city without Him, we are asking to be knocked out. Jesus Christ is the only adequate shield. There is nothing particularly mystical about the spiritual forces at play in the city; they are a very normal part of human experience. Life here is an open battlefield. But we must be optimistic soldiers, following a Captain who wants always to keep us going and to keep us safe.

An Attitude of Love for Our Cities. In addition to our optimism about the sovereignty of God, we Christians need to work out a positive, rather than negative, image of the city. Protestantism has somehow inherited a false perspective that says, "God made the country; man made the city." Even the names of many churches bear this out: Pleasantdale Community Church, Brookside Baptist, Shady Rest Presbyterian, Mountainside Methodist. Sometimes we get so restful we give the impression of a cemetery! We smile and nod and avoid the closeness within our fellowship that discloses flaws and problems and conflicts. The appearance from the outside may very well be one of living in a trance, a dreamworld where life is unreal.

We imply by our retreats that we can find God in nature. And we do need to withdraw occasionally even as Christ did—at the ocean or the lake or in the mountains. But we imply by contrast that God has withdrawn from the city and left only a pit of snakes. We picture the city in our minds as a demonic assortment of hippies, prostitutes, junkies, gangsters, pool halls, slums, and vice dens. The city may have started with Cain, but it will climax with Christ. We need to keep in mind that the destiny of the redeemed is a city.

What about the architectural beauty that lies in the old sections of a city? What about the fascinating ethnic atmosphere? What about the vigorous spirit in the children, who have not yet been crushed by intolerance and greed? What about the beauty of skyscrapers silhouetted at dusk? Or the traffic flowing through a cloverleaf? Or the interesting people walking down the avenue? What about the gold in the mire?

I like the cadence of the jackhammer. I like the sight of a huge crane hoisting steel beams into place. I like the flow of concrete, the clacking of a million heels on the finished pavement. I like the feel of sweat, of tears, and flesh. Here is action; here is life. In the crush of multitudes, the power of the living Jesus can still be sensed. Let us not limit our spiritual experience to the Grand Canyon.

An Attitude of Love for All People. The gospel is for all. The gospel never classifies people by race, class, or social standing.

James pictures two men. One man wore a gold ring and expensive apparel. The other man, obviously poor, arrived in shabby clothes. The shortsighted usher had made class distinctions in his mind before he ever got into this spot. His quick disposal of the problem at hand placed the well-dressed worshiper in an excellent seat, and the poor man was told to sit on the floor or stand up! James teaches that respect of persons is sin (James 2:9).

The inclusive gospel cannot be shared by exclusive people. To label people as worthy and unworthy, as good and bad, as acceptable and repulsive is not consistent with the grace of God. Both are thoroughly anti-Christian. In Jesus Christ there is neither Jew nor Greek, bond nor free, male nor female. Classism and racism are insults to God. Every man, regardless of outward differences, is made in the image of God. God's love included Philemon and Onesimus; Nicodemus and the Samaritan woman. A great church must include all people, regardless of background. In studying the life of John Wesley, it is